THE BEGINNING...
THE END...
ANEW!

ZEDART HODGES

THE BEGINNING...
THE END...
ANEW!

An Autobiography

ReadersMagnet, LLC

The Beginning... The End... ANew!
Copyright © 2020 by Zedart Hodges

Published in the United States of America
ISBN Paperback: 978-1-952896-37-8
ISBN Hardback: 978-1-952896-38-5
ISBN eBook: 978-1-952896-39-2

All rights reserved. No part of this publication may be reproduced, stored in a retrieval system or transmitted in any way by any means, electronic, mechanical, photocopy, recording or otherwise without the prior permission of the author except as provided by USA copyright law.

The opinions expressed by the author are not necessarily those of ReadersMagnet, LLC.

ReadersMagnet, LLC
10620 Treena Street, Suite 380 | San Diego, California, 92131 USA
1.619.354.2643 | www.readersmagnet.com

Book design copyright © 2020 by ReadersMagnet, LLC. All rights reserved.
Cover design by Ericka Obando
Interior design by Shemaryl Tampus

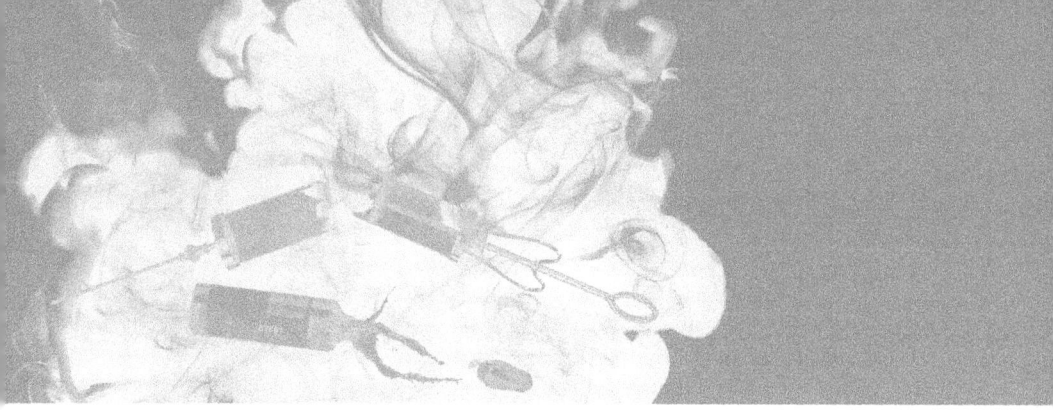

CONTENTS

PART 1

Check This Out 7

I swear on my seed. 11

Wisdom 12

What a Visit 14

PART 2

Drugs 22

The Eternal Curse from Birth 23

Peace 24

Playing with Forever. 28

It's Not Easy 30

It's Like That 33

I Am Not Ready 34

Commit to Doing Good Deeds 36

Let's Make It Right 39

We need boundaries. 43

Faith. 45

PART 3

Thank You, Lord.. 58

Conversations. 59

Look At This 61

Remember 63

Freedom 65

I am not a Slave 66

Transforming our Minds 69

The Plight Deepens 71

Let's pray for the Father 73

Spirituality is a way of life.. 74

About the Author 76

The Attack on the Mind 77

God's Love 80

Closing Remarks 81

Security 83

PART 4

The Ten Commandment Paraphrase 93

Stand Firm 96

Prayer for Strength 99

A few words of wisdom from the author. 103

PART 5

Let's Pray 112

The God of this World. 114

Dangerous Position. 117

It Starts at Home 120

Let's pray. 124

What Must the Church Say? 129

Get Free 130

Top of the Pile 131

Thank you Lord Save Our Children..................132

Our Default Position at Conception 135

Passing the Torch 136

I was Crippled.....................................137

The Cycle Must Be Broken 139

PART 1

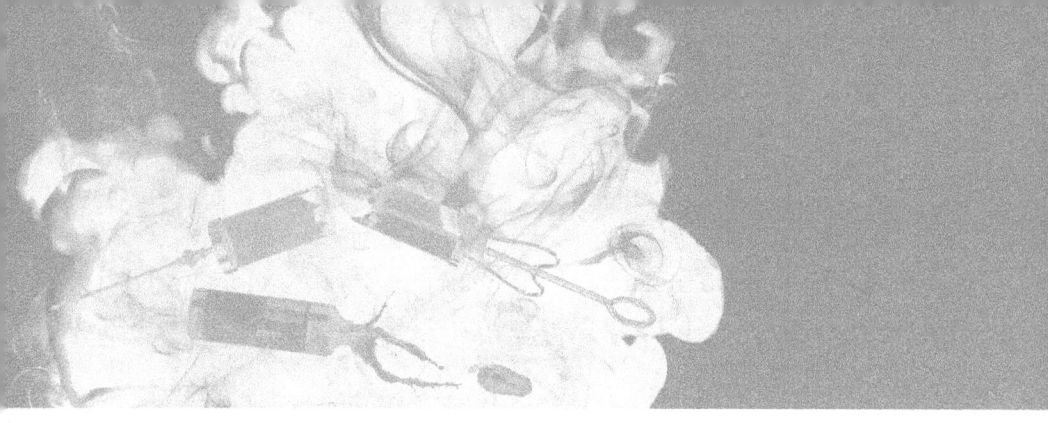

I'VE KIND OF LOOKED BACK on my life and reflect on how things are better now. All these structures and it's something every one of us needs - structure from our youth as you must start early. without it, it can be a little rough. That was the least of the things I thought I needed. There was this young man that one time said that one has got to know his limitations. So with the help of God and the love of Christ along with thy guidance of the Holy Spirit, I was Blessed to pin these notes. It's called...

Conversations with self. Alone.
Along the way.

I was sitting around with no special task in mind, just meditating on the Savior and I thought what is it that makes people afraid of change. It's like all you have to do is read the manual on how to do it. The task is just to respect me and my son and in return, I'll give you an everlasting life. There is no test, all you need to do is ask for my help when it seems that you can't hold it in. Another thing, is you need to understand the order in which I operate because that's what I'm about as well

Let's pray

Father help me to understand the character of your living. I need you to help me identify behind God the Father, the Son, and the Holy Spirit, to also help me with living right in Jesus' name.

Do you remember when you started a new job or whatever your employer had to show you how to perform well. It's the same way with being saved. People of the Church need to show you the past of the church to help you understand. Through bible study and Sunday mass, this will give you examples of trust and hearing his word for your faith. Increasing your salvation is a gift of grace. Through faith

Failure to depend on God or resist His word is to grieve the Spirit. Heaven's grace trains us how to live on earth so you really have nothing to worry about. Just make an effort let me tell you what may help you understand this book of life as you read this way. First I would like for you to focus your attention on the Book of John. Then the book of Act's, then go to Matthew, Mark, Luke, John, Acts, and so on to the book of Revelation's. I think this will help.

You better understand the outcome of this spiritual war that has already been won but we still have to fight and we will win as long as we remember who is in charge. Now we will lose a fight or two but we still know that the spiritual fight is won. I almost forget every time before starting to read the Bible, I pray and ask the Lord for knowledge, wisdom, and understanding. In Jesus name if you do as I did and put as much effect in studying God's word and as you did when you're making an escape. Those drugs you will do just fine. Trust me now when you first started this journey with God, it seem funny because God is invisible. But he's real and you will see if you study him with a pure heart I know you say with a pure heart and I say you can do this. Just ask him for

THE BEGINNING... THE END... ANEW!

help but we must worship him in Spirit and truth, some of us may have a problem with one of both of these. Again ask the Lord for help the way I handled this monkey on my back was, first, I was determined to get clean. And stay clean. As this journey began I was more and more determined to make this thing work for me. I knew that I wasn't meant to do this as most of my friends were dead in jail, there were less and less so-called friend's around and that all they wanted was another hit. I pray that this book will help somebody that wants to do better. Now, this won't work unless you really want it for you, not mom or dad or sister or girlfriend. This has to be walked by no one but you and the Lord will only help you if you ask him. It takes time and change isn't just going to happen.

I know that a lot of people think that they are intellectually all-knowing but according to the word of God, the fool say's in his heart there is no God. Now the finite mind of man can't even begin to understand the limitations of man more less the workings of the God. Knowing God also mean having an experience with God. The wholeness of God is to change your way of thinking, your way of life. We need the one that created our life. I am happy that the Lord blessed me with the wisdom to convey this knowledge of overladen wisdom to share with those that would appraise their lives. As more than the same total amount of drugs that you can put in your arm or your nose, all I'm trying to convey is give you an even chance without the benefit of a mind-blowing buffer bug that comes with helping somebody.

Now when you make that wonderful move and accept Jesus as your Lord and savior. After you get saved just remember believers can't be demon-possessed and you can be influenced by demon's. Only true friends likened from the first time you accepted Jesus Christ as Lord. However as soon as you accept Christ as Lord those demons will start coming around to try to help you make up your mind not to do what is right. That's Satan's way of thinking and acting to control us, so you know one of the most important things is you can do for you is just listen and start thinking good thoughts and also start changing your moral conduct and speech. So really, being a Christian is like changing our old clothes for a new suit and all you need to do is to clean up and be an obedient son or daughter. It's really just that simple.

Now there's another thing that one must do to justify ourselves as well as qualify the nation from the formidable evil. One also needs to understand the origin of the battle which will determine or dictate the need for salvation. As well as accountability that is paramount if we are to have a profound encounter with Christ. When we foster a relationship with Christ, we will traiblaze through and the spiritual will become more and more ablaze for the word of God and the authority of Christ will reveal the absolutes of what Christianity is all about. Now pray on this and say to the Lord to allow the Holy Spirit to teach us as we study his word all in Jesus name.

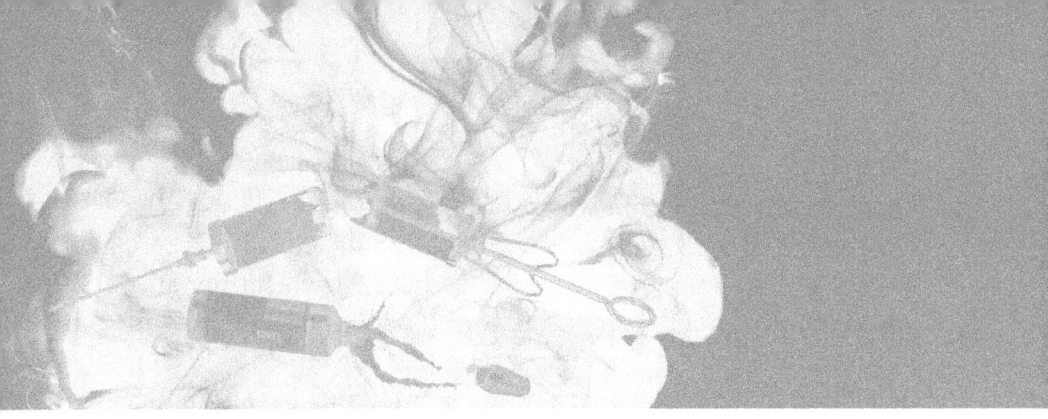

CHECK THIS OUT

Eventually the restraint of the Holy Spirit which limits the operation of sin in the world as well as one's life. But in a little while, God's grace will lay hold on those rebellious souls that think it's all about them. But little by little while reality will stretch your mind to the breaking point and as you will react or undergo a chemical change in your body, your mind will begin to collapse physically and mentally and this you may realize that the end is near. Now unless there is intervention, no announcement is needed. Life takes a sudden turn and knocks us flat but for most the jolt awakens us and we suddenly remember that God is in control but we need a relationship with Jesus Christ.

Everybody knows God but nobody trusts Jesus and that's what we must do off the top. You must go from a violent rebel to being captured at will. Another glorious conversion of a notorious sinner.

Let me go back and touch on this subject again, it's called boundaries. I believe that because there were no boundaries a lot of people created bounties. We know that there are laws making it mandatory in this social system, based on some government control. There must be boundary and in some cases I think that they were not strict as far as some people are concerned. The concept of incarceration was conceived and in some cases the cutting off of one's foot wasn't enough. You were cut off from society and from my experience this is about the worst thing that could happen other than extinction. How we know that with incarceration there is guaranteed time to study God's word thus beholding the men you put in prison are standing in the Church teaching its people.

You see, all of us have emotions and feelings that both are part of us, at least they shouldn't define us. That's why I believe we have a degenerate society because we have or we are regulated by our distribution reoccurrence of arrogance towards everything. We need to put a thermostat on both of those threats and befriend the Creator's Son as most of us need to change our surroundings, change our pace, our lifestyle. We need to pause and remember the remarkable and radical transformation that was done on our behalf at the beginning. I am Jesus whom you are persecuting my Father, help me in Jesus name.

We by chance build a wall of mistrust and we don't want anyone to try and cross over with anyone or anything that might change our focus attention. I found that it's very hard when we don't have any parents to guide or help us. The least to grow physical moreover spiritually because some didn't know Jesus Christ. Either the blind will be leading the blind and whenever you do not decide to become one of the sons of God, we as a people must to realize who God is and be a man or woman enough to accept Christ.
The best way to do for me was to ask questions as I read the word of God. Faith is trust and the only way that your trust will increase is that you forget about the things that you heard from other folks, and read the bible for yourself. I said this before, pray before you read the word of God and thank him afterwards.
This thing about being out on your own, I realize that this was the savior speaking. Also, I am pretty sure all things will start

to come together for you and whoever else that wants something better for themselves. As you begin to understand after a prayer is said asking for knowledge wisdom and understanding

Father

As I study your word help me to understand your will and purpose of my life. I am asking you for knowledge and wisdom and understanding.

When someone introduces you to the savior, some people will admire you for studying the book of life and most will be glad for what you have chosen. But still a lot won't understand not knowing that we were compelled by God to study the character of self, which would have been a distant dream unless one is cultivated in periods of time spent in solitude and quietness and obscurity.

You know shooting dope popping pills only softens the blow of the potholes you run over during your travel down the road of self-destruction.

Now you need to change the picture to fit the frame. But there must be the gift of grace fixed in one's life so that when the duel begins, you will stand firm like when you would. Go to the dope man to remember how to determine who you were. There was this one guy I know I had such a talk, like a parable that blows the horns off. Like a Billy goat if you listen to him long enough.

You would be prone to think and believe anything. But thank God that he introduced me to Jesus. Now I still stumble but each time that I did, I got back up and I got stronger and in a little while I didn't stumble anymore. It felt good not to wake up sick. We must know that the word of God gives us strength and that's the real deal. Trust me there are a lot of people outside the arena of mercy.

With the circle of grace, there will always be friends. Along with other people that will try to hinder the progress you are wanting, just pray and ask the Lord to remove anyone or anything that's trying to hinder you from it. Studying his word and living right the Father helped me study without being hindered by anyone or anything in Jesus name.

There's nothing that you can know that's never been known. There's nothing that you can see that's never been seen. As you trip into the bible's life-giving power, as bad as it can be the nature of God is to forgive and with the assurance of grace, only then our relationship with the creator is restored.

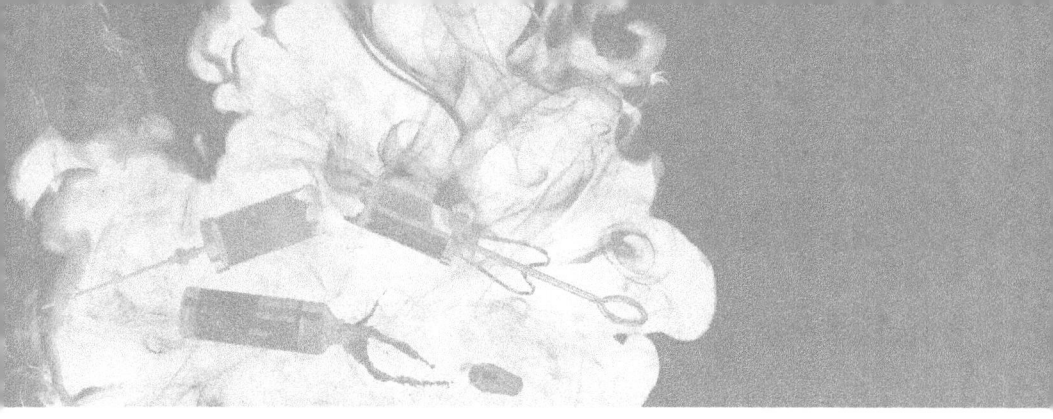

I SWEAR ON MY SEED.

THIS WAS A VERY POPULAR phrase in the joint back in the day and maybe even now. But as I reflect on what this phrase is really saying I say wow not because of the person or whoever expressed it but this is one of God's ways of procreation. I don't think that people really realize what they are saying or the meaning behind it. Check this out, we are in a spiritual warfare both in and out of the body of Christ. Both the chosen and the unchosen, it doesn't matter, the Bible says that Satan comes to steal, kill and destroy. It doesn't matter if you are in Christ or out. Now if you swear on your seed, that's what Satan wants. You got you to say Lord I thank you for giving me strength to overcome in the name of Jesus.

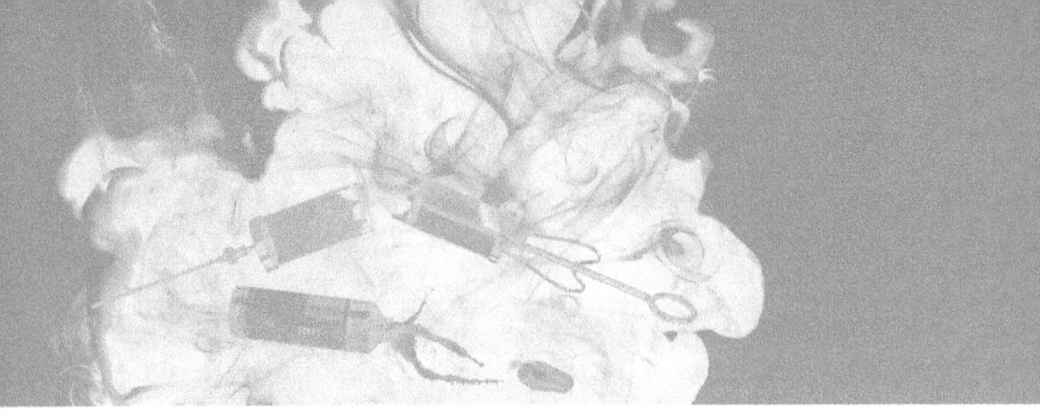

WISDOM

I BELIEVE THAT GOD'S WISDOM IS his main purpose for us. I also think that his wisdom evades those who predestines themselves for whatever reason like they got it going on and a lot of people forget that his wisdom does not operate outside of his purpose. That's why I think that when you plan something for outside of his purpose it won't work. I am glad we have a wise God who put it all together instead of leaving it all up to us.

Let me tell you about God's wisdom. This happened to me some time ago, but I still remember it like it was yesterday when I stood my ground after receiving the light. I was facing twenty or so years, and I talked to God like I am talking to you. I told him all that I had done or all I could remember and after prayed to him in Jesus name. I left out of the courtroom with only fifty-seven months. Now that's God's truth, you can't mix human wisdom and divine wisdom. If so, all you are is a sophisticated person sounding so ignorant.

Any discussion about God's character, we must not omit this ongoing concept which may be said about a typical father who warns his kids of impending danger. One may say he's not a good dad, his compassion for you would be in question. You would say

THE BEGINNING... THE END... ANEW!

he doesn't care about me but those that knew better might say he's just scared. He always wanted us to take care of our self and one another.

Lord help me to take care of my family, keep your loving arms around us help us to never be alienated from each other and always keep you first in our lives in Jesus name.

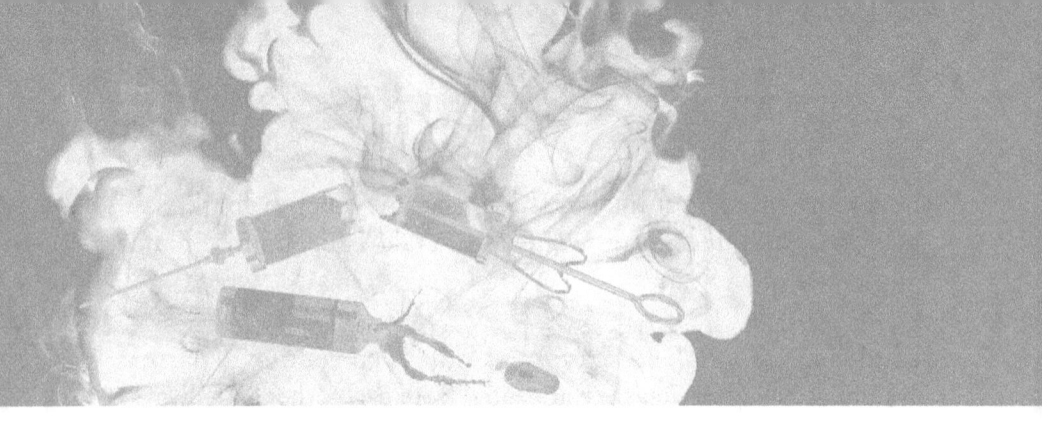

WHAT A VISIT

A FEW MONTHS AGO THE LORD blessed me to visit the motherland of Nairobi in Kenya. I went with my wife where she's from. I was like a kid in a candy store and had a pretty good time meeting my in-laws. Although for some folks it may not have been so good but I had a nice time as we visited the animal orphanage outside Nairobi. There we went to see the boas of Kenya and these are villages which houses are very old inside and out. There was living area, cooking area, as well as sleeping areas that are replicas of each tribe which lived around the East African country. From there you can see where the embassy stood and I was impressed with a lot of things that I saw. From the famous Jomo Kenyatta's airport and its skyscraper. I wanted to go back to Nairobi as we also need to visit Mombasa.

A misconception about Africa is that everybody wants to be in control but nobody or only a few want to go through the right process. A lot of folks want to leapfrog into power. If you look hard enough, you'll see this in a lot of countries. I guess you just have to say, just like any other places. One would be right about America that it took them a while and most of other countries are just getting started.

THE BEGINNING... THE END... ANEW!

Like the glory that's Lebanon. Its trees, like the wisdom of Solomon and his kingly splendor has led to the downfall of man. I believe this will be manifested to perfection if one is playing God.

There's only one to turn to for you to be saved, there is only one God, no other. He created the universe and man. Everybody knows God and that's a good thing but we need to be able to trust in Jesus. It's like in the Bible, it cites that those who denies the Son and the Father, is like being friends with somebody who don't like your son or daughter.

Once upon a time there was this big man that owned everything. He had it all. Then there was this other guy that thought that he could take something from the man. He had a few people that ran with him and he formed a gang and they tried to take what this other man had not knowing that people loved this big man. Anyway he found out about this and told this guy to a battle. A fight took place and the little guy got kicked out. He ran out of town and they came to this other place not knowing that the big man also owned the place.

The devil, as a snake talked to this young lady and he twisted what the big man had told them of a forbidden fruit that they were not to eat. But the lady grew inquisitive so she ate it partaking the fruit with her companion. After a while they heard the big man walking in the garden. The man was afraid, was naked and he hid from the big man. He said, who told you to eat the forbidden fruit? The little man said it was the woman. The blame game started and that very instant the big man said to the woman how could you do this to me then she said the snake tricked me.

The Lord will help us not to be tricked by anything or anybody in Jesus name. Now I'm about to paraphrase for a little bit. The Lord said to Satan okay, let the games begin but in the end, I will win. I will use the worst of you to talk to the best of you. This is also important because even though we as believers cannot be demon-possessed, we can be influenced. Most of us do allow Satan's way of thinking to control us. My point is that behind nations and events there is angelic activity's that overrides the natural standard and reputation of self.

Remember this, no matter what happens to you in life or as a result of entering into spiritual warfare, even if you are despairing for your very life, you can always be assured that you are the center of our God's love and guardianship.

Father

In the name of Jesus give me strength, to always be mindful of your word and your glorious will for my life in the name of Jesus.

Adam forfeited eternal life by choosing Satan's tree of the knowledge of good and evil over God's tree of life. The real war against humanity started when our enemy first questioned God's integrity and love. His creation is clothed in God's glory but we are also stripped naked by our desire to sin continually. Some people don't care to be covered so they hid from God while they fell deeper and deeper into the misguided strategy of depression brought on by the loss of passion for the creator. We also tend to fool ourselves into thinking that this is normal but contrary to popular belief this is a slow death of mind and body.

Lord God, keep me in my right mind. Christians are to grow by feeding themselves with hearing acting and doing the word of God. If you meet someone and ask them, are you saved? They may say no I am spiritual and have the wrong answer. Again there is someone else and you ask them do you love Jesus and they say I respect him. From the wrong answer they then ask what's the difference and you say God gave all his power when he raised him from the dead.

Now, believers are described as one who has turned to idols to serve the living God. From Jesus Christ they then say but everybody is a child of God ok no wrong answer everybody is God's creation but you must accept Jesus Christ as your Lord and savior, only then you will become his child. While this doctrine is rejected by some, others find it of great spiritual value to accept without any question the Biblical teaching of Christianity.

Another truth that lead me to the savior is that I read somewhere where it says that if you confess to the Lord Jesus to believe in your heart that God raised him from the dead you will be saved. To believe in your heart but when you are in the hospital and can't speak, what then?

Great fighters are not great because they can throw a lot of punches but they are great because they can take a lot and still win the battle. Now with this spiritual battle, you just need to step into the ring and listen to the referee. We also need to have someone that fought him spiritually to show us how to win. And you are right, you can worship God with singing, praying and teaching his word to those we can do outside of the church.

As a child of God, as a Christian, as a member of the church, I have the privilege of worshipping God. To worship as an attitude of the heart and spirit every child who is also physically able should attend the assembly of the Church to worship God.

Chris Oyakhilome Christ Embassy
1-800-869-3557

Weekly
888-372-3453
1-888-7685627
800
1 888 3723453
1 800-7685627
708

ncesc.com

PART 2

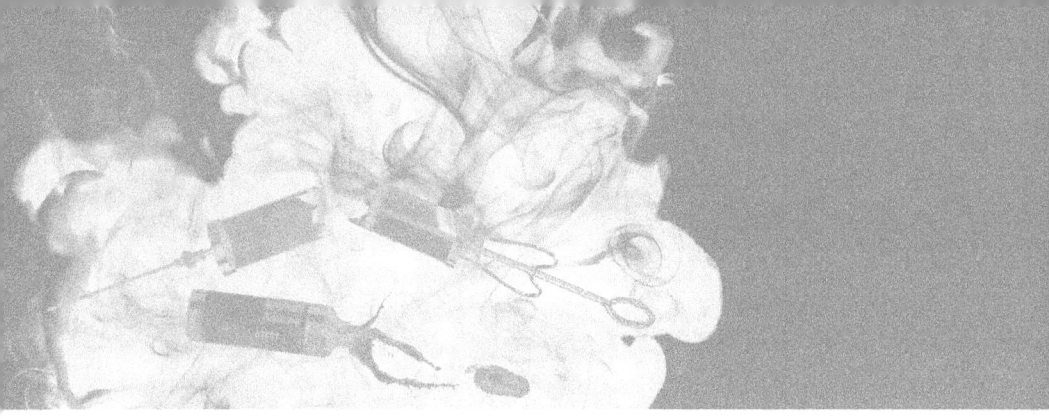

There may and most of the time be little tidbits of info here but I assure you that this is the way it's supposed to be. But I've found that when you are trying to escape from the clutches of addiction any addiction your mind becomes a battleground and more often than not we usually focus our attention on the thing that offer's the least bit of effort on our part. Would you agree there's an old saying that says you better be careful who you know who has that Willie Lynch syndrome. That itself is crazy but withdrawal from drugs, you are setting yourself up for a killing. Let's just focus on self for now.

The strongman is just waiting for us to start stretching our mind, there can be little thoughts of self-worth, self-will and a sense of doubt as the will keeps invading our weak minds. We are to be ever mindful that we are trying to beat this way of thinking right.

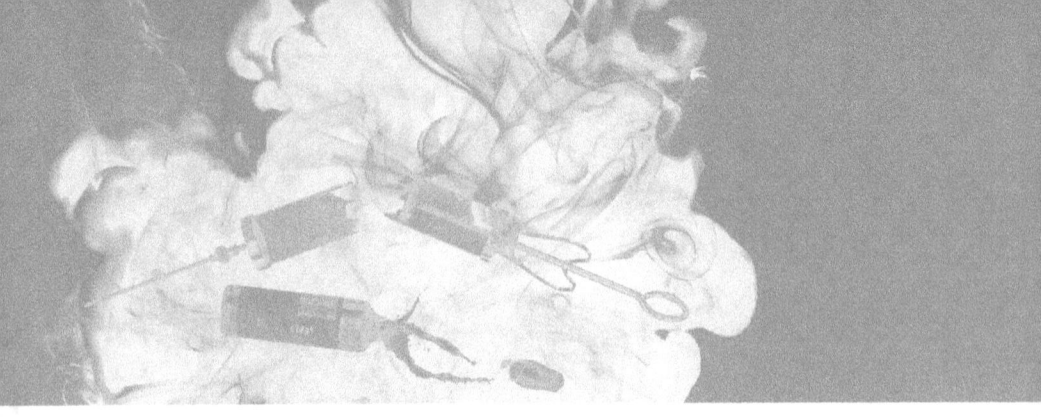

DRUGS

A SUBSTANCE USED IN THE DIAGNOSIS or prevention of a disease or as a component of a medication. Such a substance as recognized or defined by the US Food Drug and Cosmetic Act causing changes in behavior and often addiction.

Drug Abuse

Habitual use of drugs to alter one's mood emotion or state of consciousness.

Thank you, father, I know that you are the author and finisher of my faith and I thank you for deliverance. Father I want to stop this madness in my life. I know that it is wrong and I want to stop but every time I try to stop it seem as if people and things start happening that seem so effortless on my part. I mean, it seems like all I need to do is be in place and then when the thought or I do passes of wanting to do many things to stop happening. So I need your help to be strong when this happens and anything that will hinder me from doing the right thing. It seems like I don't have the strength to do right on my own so Father, help me in the name of Jesus. Thank you.

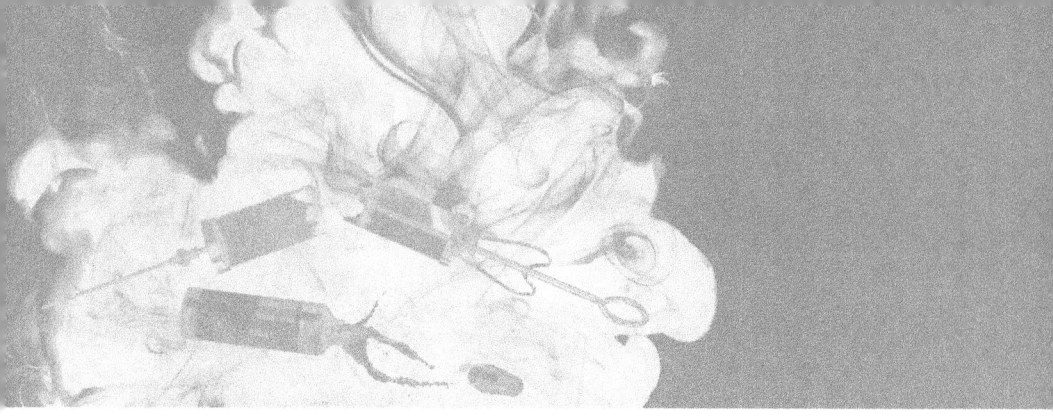

THE ETERNAL CURSE FROM BIRTH

Help us, Father, to overcome we need to see yourself as being free. The Illusion of a dream will allow you to be what you want to be but the reality of Christ will help you make them come true.

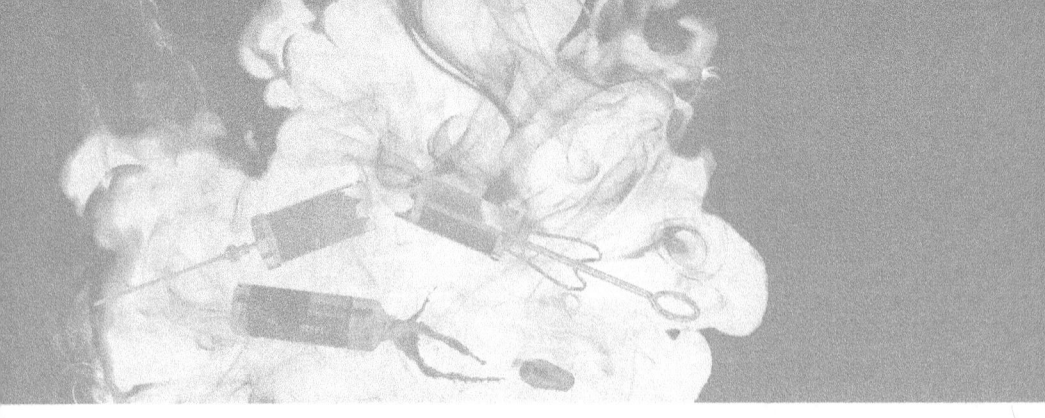

PEACE

I KNOW THAT A LOT OF people don't believe in God but hear this, he's you only ticket out. With a clean mind body and soul hear this, the thing is everybody I know, I want you to understand this, there are very few people that trust in Jesus Christ and all he wants is for you to make him Lord in your life. I just want to let you know how I trusted in the Lord to give me strength to overcome. I am not saying that all your days will be sunny and bright, I don't want you to even think that but I can promise that he will give you the strength to overcome if you don't give up and give in to him as your partner.

The rabbit still got the gun and he went to keep it until you gain enough strength to see who the rabbit is and keep him at bay.

I just want to help my brothers and sisters that think that there is no hope that life is evading them and their friends are avoiding them now. In a lot of cases that's true, life passes you by because you chose to stand still with that drug of choice and think that no one will notice you shying away from life. Your friends let you off because they fear hanging with you will also label them as being a loser like you going nowhere fast. In life there are arguments by design for and against anything even life itself and the existence of God.

I know that life will give you the chances you need. You realize in your mind that there's a better way not from man but for man now. I need for you to believe this unless there's a transformation of the heart for self and know that we can be anything we want. To be clean, we must make up our mind that we must know that there's something bigger, that has our best interest at heart other than the dealer.

There's a lot of people that I need to give thanks. Those that know me before and them that know me now. Most of all, to the keeper of my soul for when I was out there strung out like a research monkey, wanting to get off the merry go round, He gave me strength. To give him praise and thank him. He allowed me to see myself free. Now I believe that freedom from self can only come about if the desire to be free is not there from the beginning.

We are the most intellectual creatures that God has put on the passing of time. We have taken our eyes of the Creator and fasten them on objects of our desire. We must be mindful of which God we are talking about. That's just something that I thought I would throw out there.

Peace

The will to win is not nearly as important as the will to prepare to win.

There will be times when you will think that everybody and everything is against you and what you are trying to do for yourself. Now that you've made up your mind to begin to do the right thing, we must also realize that our ways and thinking are not back to normal. Even we would question the smallest of matters, you will probably say, am I the only one that's thinking like this. Trust me, everybody would think this very thing at first but as we get back to normal and the right way of thinking. We will begin to notice how things will start to fall in place and as we began this journey, you will start to see that people are pulling for you. Even them, they don't really care to much for you. People that you have hurt in the past and everything. But remember, nobody owes us anything but respect and as they see us doing the right thing, this to will come. Trust me.

You know through this journey of soberness in which you are trying to obtain, that can only be done through your will and the choice you make in the positive. There's no "we" in clean, there's only you. Everyone loves to see you fail, wants to see you in this mellow madness of self-destruction. Everyone around you that don't really care for you, they really want to see you fail. Again, there's no one on Earth that should value your life more than you now. When you begin to see things and situations around you change for the better, you start to change with them. Look, no one can help you but you. Even God will not change you against your will, you also need to believe that you can do this. You need to know that you can transform you. This is, first and foremost, to start this transformation of self and in time you and your life will begin to change for the better. You must behave. This I know that you get tired of waking up in the morning and trying to figure out where that next hit will come from. Think about that.

Checks this, I am not trying to sway or convert nobody. All I am trying to do is let everybody know that what worked for me. Also, there's a whole new swagger that will begin to dictate your ability to convey and make know the real you.

Freedom isn't free to say it loud. Freedom isn't free. That's right. Now let that sink in for a few okay. That's enough

THE BEGINNING... THE END... ANEW!

Now

Freedom is liberty from slavery exempt from bondage. We were created to be rulers but somehow, overtime we have or we're ruled by less than nothing. This world is trying hard to take us away from our roots, our way of life and especially our God, and that's real.

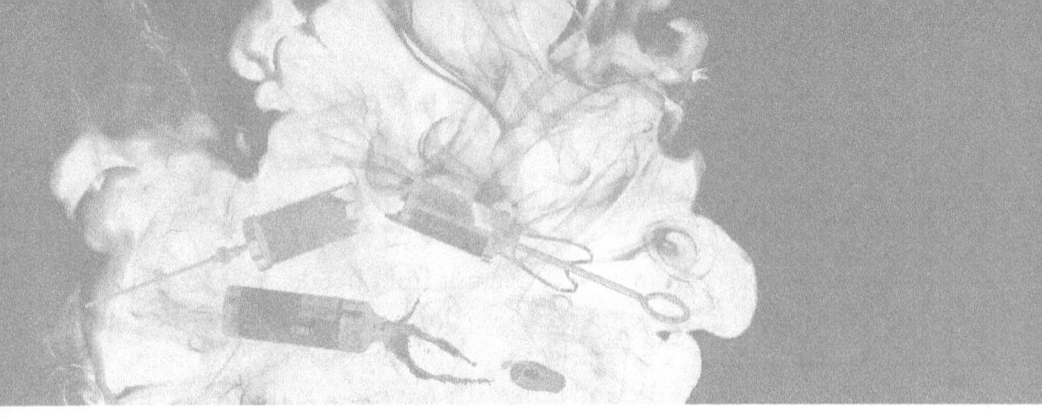

PLAYING WITH FOREVER

There's a lot of things that I have encountered over the years, believing in God isn't one of them. Also, over the passing of time, I've heard people tend to veer away from the supremacy of the almighty. We must understand that no matter what, he loves us and this is that security of the believer.

Now most of us, especially those that know of God but don't know Jesus as Lord, often question why God allows bad things to happen. Well, with God he can do what he wants to do according to his word. There's no one up there with him that he has to answer to. No one. Also we are to accept Jesus as Lord and until we do, our Father will allow what he wants to happen. God is our spiritual father, Jesus is our brother and the Spirit is that wisdom inside of us that we don't always listen to even though we know that he told us the truth.

THE BEGINNING... THE END... ANEW!

You think I was just a man
You think I don't love you
You think that I don't forgive
You don't call me
You don't love me
You don't respect me
You don't know me
You have forgotten me
You stopped following me
As your parents did
You have other gods
And you say
Why do I allow things to happen?
Really?

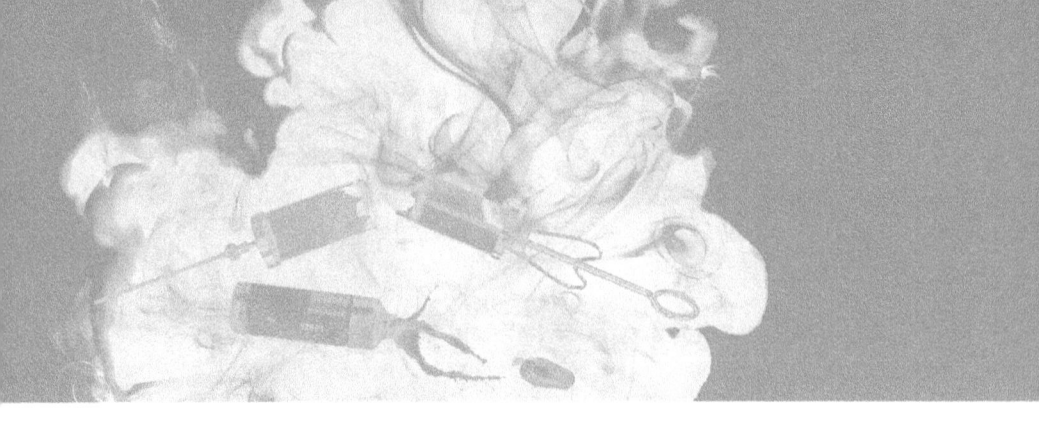

IT'S NOT EASY

This journey that you are about to take for yourself will be a little hard at first but as time go on, and you begin to see things that will happen with a clear mind, the more excited you will be about being free. Freedom.

There will be times when you will think that everybody and everything is against you. The goal that you are trying with the help from the Lord are waiting for you to obtain. For you and yours. When you began to realize that its coming closer, you get more things despite the fiendish thoughts entering your mind. When you start to reach your goal and believe that it is possible and obtainable we must continually ask the Lord for strength. For you and the people that you love and hurt in the past, it will begin to pull for you to beat this thing.

We must remember that we did this to ourselves. When we refuse to be accountable to our parents. Now, most of us were raised in a single-parent home. That parent was often than likely the mother and more often than not, she thought that like most woman, she doesn't need a man around. She fails to realize that boys need their father, girls need their fathers. Because believe it or not, everybody needs to be accountable. It may sound crazy but it's true, you know this.

THE BEGINNING... THE END... ANEW!

Chastisement at the hand of God is the expectation of every true child of God.

Think of this one for a minute. There are a lot of things that we, as an intolerable people like. We sometimes need to get away and we even need to get away from our self, because we are our own worst enemy at times.

When I was out there shooting drugs everyday, mainly heroin and crack, I knew of God but I was afraid of a real relationship with him. Also know that I needed to make an 180 turn in my life if I wanted to keep living, I just was unable muster up the strength within myself to make this happen. Now I know that there are a lot of people out there that fool themselves by thinking that they can do something about their condition on their own. Well, all I can say is you need to stop tricking yourself into believing this falsehood because it's nothing but old fashion denial. You can't beat this thing and the only way you can get good spiritual assistance is from God, through Jesus Christ. Also I know that a lot of people don't want to hear this but what can I say, I am telling you the truth. I shoot heroin and crack together for a long time so I know what you will be going through and trust me, it isn't any fun when the rabbit got the gun.

When you start feeling better about yourself, getting clean when you start caring about the things that's going on around you. And you begin paying attention to the news or you start to notice all the craziness that's everywhere. Especially when it comes to people being mistreated for nothing, you wonder what happened was I so into myself that I forgot about the righteousness of being right and stop seeing thing's for what it is instead. What it could do, drugs make me forget about the realization of living and piling me into a world of unrealistic betrayal of friends and family. Did drug really dos this or was it there from the beginning? I just needed an excuse to show people how I felt instead of locating people to help me with my insight of how the world really is well. I'm afraid so but help is on the way. Peace.

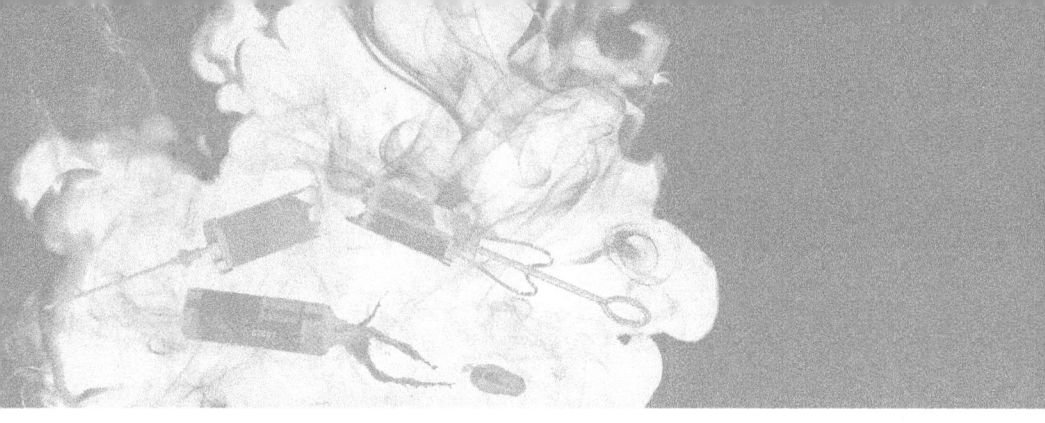

IT'S LIKE THAT

WHEN TIME HAS ELAPSED ON what you think is the end, it is only the beginning. If you are truly interested in finding yourself and understand that it will take more than who you think you know on this earth to help you on this journey of getting your mind, body, and soul back to where you think it is supposed to be.

Nothing is ever easy, there's only good or bad but bad isn't better. It's just that when you allow situations to play out in your life, especially when you don't want to be accountable to anything or anybody. Other than that, which we give most of or all our attention to, no matter who or what it maybe. I am speaking from a natural standpoint that can't get it twisted.

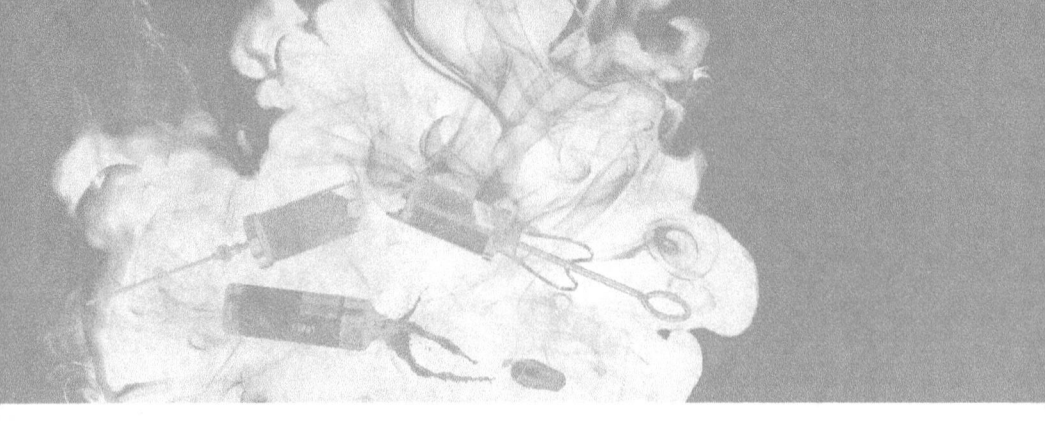

I AM NOT READY

A LOT OF TIME'S I SPEAK to my brothers and sisters about a real relationship with God and most don't really understand that I am talking about the existence of God. Now, if we start a conversation, we can get into the attributes of God. But a lot of people have not knowingly experienced his love and I believe that this may be one of the many reasons why they would say I am not ready. And most likely no one has explained to them about salvation and the rewards of being renewed by his word. I don't think that no one has explained to them that having a relationship with God is only the beginning of forever, some would say my father or my mother is saved or a preacher so I think they have enough religion for both of us. Come on, do you really believe this? So is the rabbit gone keep the gun. Another one is when I stop doing this or that, when I'll give my life to God or start going to church. He knows that you smoke, he knows you still do whatever he just wants to help you with cleaning up your mind, your body. He wants to be Lord of your life. He wants to show you that you don't need all that foolishness in your life to be accepted. That's right, I said it and thought the same way at one time but I was thinking about the creature instead of the having mine on the creator. A lot of people act interested toward the word of God but is not really concerned about the Gospel. God hears all prayers but only acts on those that carry his son's name.

The fact of the matter is that we think that we can rule God. We want to have thing's our way. This ain't no fast food. That world isn't going to happen.

When people have a negative experience with religion or church, they think that all places of worship or a particular group thinks that are all alike. All that God wants for them is for drugs kept away tucked in the past. Now that you are moving forward a little don't let this stop you. Then there are those that say I listen to preaching sometimes. But do you have a preacher in your life? The best thing I can do is tell you that any church isn't for everybody. We must pray and ask the Lord to lead you to a church now and don't neglect going to church. Until this happens, just go to different churches until the Lord gives you one where you feel confident. That this one is the one. Like the way you would choose a girl, only you got the Lord helping you. You can't lose

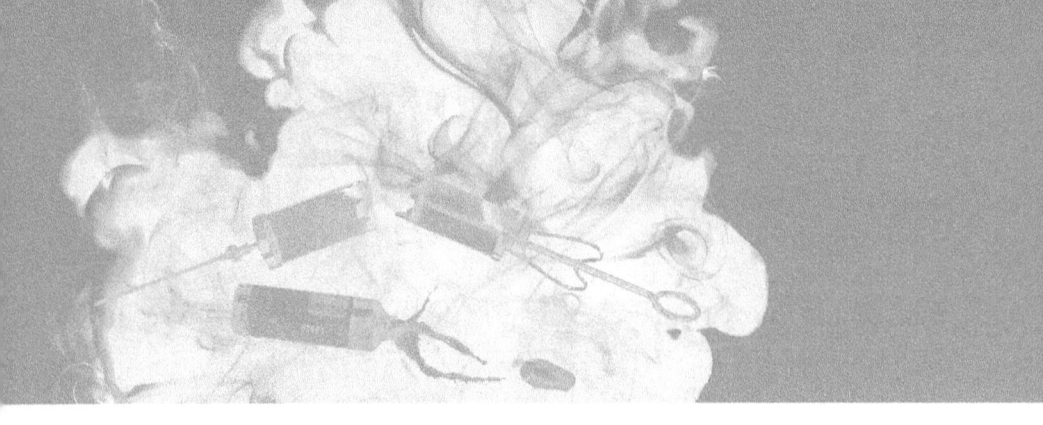

COMMIT TO DOING GOOD DEEDS

Some people think that this is enough. Well what can I say, you can do good deeds for God. In the name of Jesus or you can do good deeds for Satan.

Conscience is an inherent awareness of the difference between what is right and what is wrong. Do you rule your conscience, or do your conscience rule you? Most people I know are engaged in the former and not the latter.

Brother's we have lost our voice. We often wonder why our voice as being head of the house doesn't carry as much or any weight. Well, we have become our child's best friend instead of their parents. We negotiate rather than negate, we don't see nor you can't have enough of children's need for boundaries.

There will at the end still be those people that will not allow themselves to even think of the one true God. Even though they will see death standing next to them. When I was out there shooting dope, sometimes two or three times a day, I would think about death and dying with a needle in my arm wanting so bad

THE BEGINNING... THE END... ANEW!

to stop. But the power of the addiction and the love for the high overpowered my desire for anything and everything.

I thought I had to do this to exist. I was doing what use to be called speed-ball this was heroin and cocaine and sometime when I couldn't find cocaine, I would buy me some crack and break it back down to liquid form and then mix it with my heroin. I would do this 2-3 times a day. We would steal to buy out dope. We even did this like it was a job leaving around 8 in the morning and returning round 6-7 at night. But then I got busted went to prison and there I was introduced Jesus Christ. It took a few minutes but I finally got free. Now, freedom isn't free. But to live free is so rewarding. You'll see, if you are strong enough on the journey start and stay the course.

You didn't come into this world with anybody but you think that you need someone to second your belief in somebody, or something that we all have at one time or another have struggled with. We know very little about this spiritual aspect of this life, we have questions. But we don't go anywhere or ask somebody that knows the answers. A lot of us don't want to put ourselves out there for fear of our friends saying crazy things and deep down they want to know the same thing. All you need to do is start going to Bible study where you can get all or mostly all your question's answered. God hears all prayers but will only respond, I believe, to the ones that carry his son's name.

God can't help you if you don't believe in Him. In time he can help you to believe.

Addiction not only hurts you, it helps you to perfect the art of dying while living. We must come to a place in our life where living is more important than just existing. No one can help you live but you. People that run will never be free.

Only true freedom is given by God. Jesus died for everybody, there is a lot of manuals, maps, books, and other means of getting from point A to point B. But the book that will take you to eternity most of us seldom pick it up. More less read it. God has been belittled in the minds of many by a traditional misconception of his personality that has been handed down to us from the Dark Ages. The first redemptive work of Christ is referred to in the Bible as a ransom. you should look this work up and see what it means and figure out how it applies to yourself self. We pray to deliver us from evil. With this illustration in mind it would seem peculiarly fitting in this gigantic task of restitution that God gave Jesus power to free us and Jesus gave us the power to become free.

But wait.

There is a certain confidence in self that one gains when one becomes a Christian believe that mankind, as well as womankind believes in the existence of a supreme being or beings, to whom he or she is morally responsible in some way or another. I understand that because in a sense that's as far as your mind will allow you to go, and that's okay. If you don't want to spiritually stretch your mind to know that there's only one.

Know that I am here and there is no God beside me. I put to death and I live to live, I have been wounded and I will heal and no one can deliver out of my hands.

You see knowing God is not an option and to have a relationship with Jesus is mandatory. Your affections should be supremely set upon God and your desire for a relationship with Jesus Christ should be personalized.

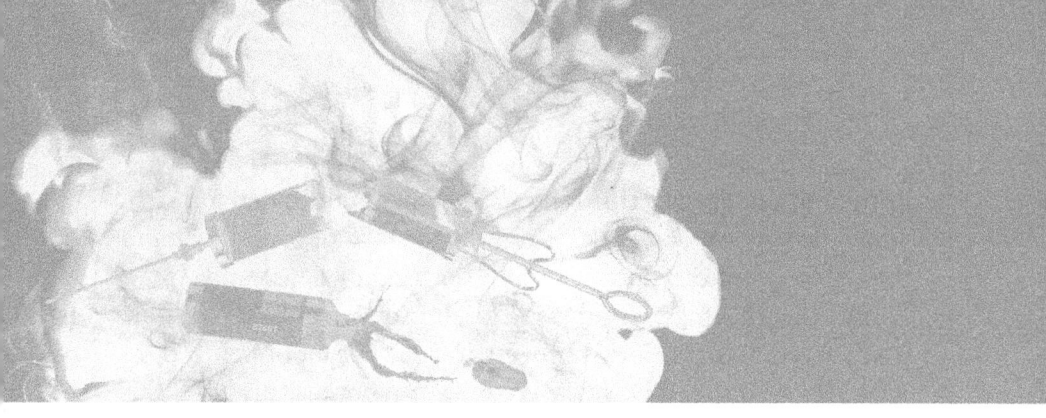

LET'S MAKE IT RIGHT

Jesus, I don't know you. I only know of your Father and I didn't know that I needed a personal relationship with you to give me strength and help me grow closer to you. I really don't know how to form a friendship with you so you are going to have to help me with this. God, put someone in my life that will help me know you. I thank you very much.

Love _ _ _ _

Now

The wonders of God is all around us. The beauty of God can be seen every day. The power of God is evident through his creation. The Ministry of God can be realized in time. The love of God can only be understood through the acceptance of his son. Look I know that you don't want to accept this fact, but that's the way it is. Truth and justice I believe is embedded in our spirit from the beginning and the only way that it will come to the forefront of our lives, I think, is that we have a change of heart and allow the truth of God to readily become our first precept for living. In this predatory world of uncertainty, the reason I think that we can't get this everlasting life is from the beginning we were born in sin and our way of thinking has been contaminated at birth. The only way we can make it right is to start all over again and the only way we can do this is to be born again, spiritually. Now, I know that this may sound crazy to some of you but get someone that's saved to explain this process to you. It's about being right with God and the only way this can come about is through Jesus Christ. It isn't about nothing somebody told you or none of that.

I remember one time back in the day I got busted and this friend of someone that I thought was my friend, we used to shoot dope together, go boasting or stealing. This one time I got busted and went to jail and this guy that I thought was my friend went to my family got the money for my bond but went and brought him some dope instead of coming to get me out of jail. Drugs will make you turn on friends and everybody that wants to help you. This friend was the rabbit with the gun.

For so long we have been a people deprived of self-worth either by groups or by our actions. So we really do these things to our self now and in doing this to our self we tend to use drugs to help us on this pity-party so we don't feel so guilty about the damage we do to self. Now, when we allow someone other than the captain of this vessel to sail with us through these waters of uncertainty, anything can and will happen. This is a sinful world but we must remember we are just visiting for some time now. I've been clean better than that since the Lord saved me from myself. Everything has not been all good but at least I have not been back out there. Now I am not saying that from time to time since I have not thought about that mellow madness.

I know that what I am about to say will be answered with an overblown sense of disbelief coupled with our flow of emotional obligation toward something that has diluted the problem at hand. Every now and then I think about the life that went through. Jesus

THE BEGINNING... THE END... ANEW!

Christ delivered me and realize that I took the gun back. I got it now but all too often we put our trust where it doesn't belong. I think that it's right but somewhere along the line we lose focus of the real deal. But then, I say whatever floats your boat even though you see a water fall up ahead. You need to be introduced to my friend, he sees where you are and want so bad to help you in times of trouble. He can help you get where you need to be clean. The will to win is not nearly as important as the will to prepare to win, we must get it right.

The illusion of dreams will let you be what you want to be. But the reality of Christ will help you make them come true. I am determined not to give-up ever again.

There's a lot of things, mentally, that will send you overboard if you allow it. That's why I believe that it's so important to ask for forgiveness from God. Without the act of forgiveness being taken, we will always experience an emptiness inside. This is not a hurting pain like you hit your leg or lump your head, this is a pain of the heart. A pain that can only be dispelled by God through Jesus Christ. Ask for forgiveness from the creator if not the action is incomplete. That emptiness will always be there if not the guilt will hinder your ability to begin the healing process. Your relationship with your self will began to foster, an illness that can only be filled spiritually. This undertaking must be developed through your heart and mind. Your desire to get clean must become paramount in your life. There are numerous other feelings that will hinder your recovery if not truly acted upon from the heart.

One of the most dangerous thing's we can do is to disconnect oneself from the creator

Everybody wants to belong to something bigger than themselves. If you happen to put your trust in something, you see that is dependency. If by chance your trust happens to be thrust on the unseen, now that's called faith. Also, there's a lot of things mentally that will send one overboard if you allow it. That's why I believe that it's so important to ask for forgiveness from God and man. We don't think about this but the pain one feels without this action being taken is not really a hurting pain like if you would hit your leg or lump your head. This pain is in your heart and can only be dispelled by God through Jesus Christ. If by chance you ask for man's forgiveness alone and the action is half-heartedly taken, it won't work. This must be asked from both parties. the guilt will only hinder your relationship that so desperately need to be formed.

There are times when we wonder about the things that happen in life especially in our house. Now, maybe it was meant to happen or maybe the situation is thrust upon us by things unseen. But sometimes I believe things happen because no one said no to disobedience, because he or she is so cute. But how many of you know that cute and disobedience will grow with you. This is why I believe so many things are upon us because no one said no about putting this in perspective. I am sure that a few times if we widen that, someone would have said no to us when we knew that we were wrong.

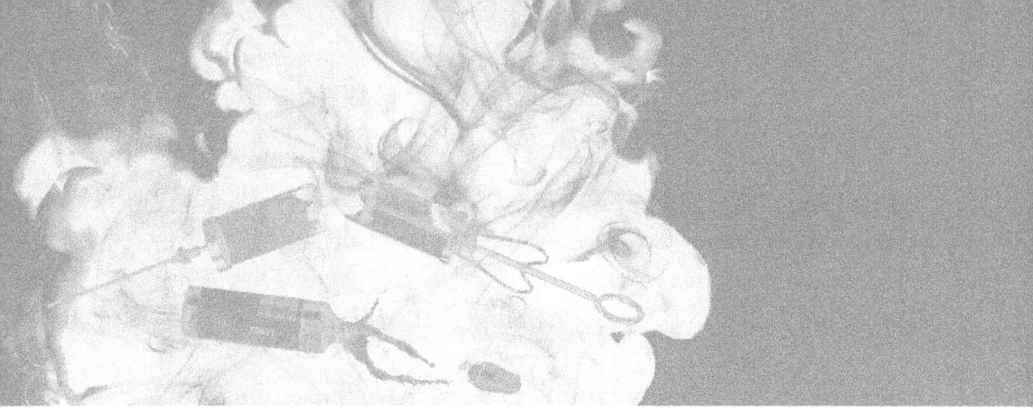

WE NEED BOUNDARIES.

I THINK THAT I KIND OF got a handle on why some people don't really want to attend church. Well, it's like this, when you hear somebody badmouth the church, pastor, or even its members, they tend to be the bearer of somebody's word. They don't want to hear God's word. Now, the word you hear from somebody, kills your spirit but the words we hear from God build's it up. That talk goes around all the time I wonder whose word they hear. Who do you have confidence in?

It's not enough to simply say who you trust you must show us or them the naysayer. All they want to do is see if you're going to hell with them. Nobody wants to go anywhere alone even hell. Growing up in a shot house there was many brothers that I thought I wanted to imitate. But as I grew older I found that all of them had flaws in their character. As I grew older and started going in and out of prison I began to see what real character tells. The most telling aspect of my venture was when I was introduced to this man Jesus and he began to show me my flaws and instilled in me the attributes of God through his character. There are many things that people think about God. But until you have met him through his son, you don't really know him or anything of his character. Now that's real.

The events that lead to greatness in a person take's place in the hidden years when few were around and no one cared. Let us never forget what life was like before Christ. Also, never- ever forget what life was like outside the boundaries of grace.

Regardless of how some people appear, they all have a past that is neither pleasant nor encouraging.

We must realize that we must believe by faith, the bible demands it. Faith to a lot of people is believing that that next shot of dope won't take them out even though they have just seen someone O.D. From an amount no bigger than the head of a dime faith to an addict is trusting that your pusher won't give you some rat poison to inject into your veins. That's faith, but it is a dead faith. The faith I want to instill in you or towards is that into everlasting life

Every now and then someone will say how do you know that he or she did or is doing something crazy. I say two reasons; one because we were born in sin and the other is because you are human. It's just our nature, the hardness of our heart is a learned action. I say action because we must stay on top of this fad but like lying, the more you do it the better you are at it. Trust me, I know.

Badness is just a state of mind. A flippant set of actions that you think will help you obtain the status you need to survive the streets of madness. Look straight through the mind. In these days of twisting, distorting, altering and compromising the truth.

Father, I pray for all those lost souls out there on some kind of maddening pursuit of self-centeredness.

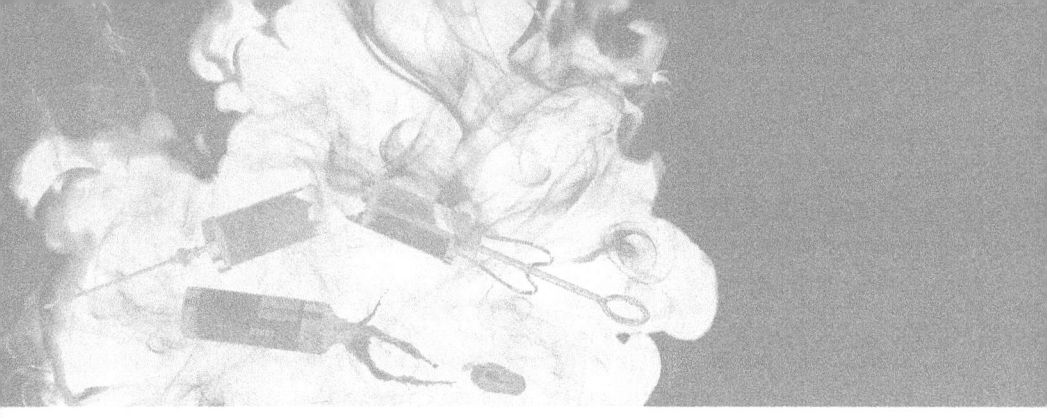

FAITH

This is an action in which everybody has a measure. I also think that it depends on one's state of mind that at any given time. But by not hearing or being affiliated with the giver of the same with one's direction, it will depend on one's level of growth. This are people who spend a lot of time and effort trying to improve themselves on the inside but not changing their behavior on the outside. God is God by himself, he can do what he wants when he wants and to whomever he wants. He will not do anything against your will. We must accept his Son in order for anything spiritual to take place in our life.

Jesus Christ became human and died sinless so that he could buy back or redeem us from our sin. Naturally as we became disconnected from him when, disobedience came on the scene back in the day. Our sin is the nature of man then began to rule.

Every part of man is hungry for something. Your body is hungry for attention. Your mind is hungry for knowledge. And your soul is homesick for a place it's never been.

Now this is not something that's been made up it's real. Have you noticed that everything that you have; money, fame, fortune and all that. But you still feel empty inside. You need Jesus.

It won't happen unless you are destined by God to have a relationship with Jesus now what that means is you can't or this won't happen unless it's done in God's way. No matter how foolish it may sound because we must remember that our ways is not his way. The things that make sense to us is not what make sense to him because we are thinking naturally when this must take place spiritually.

Man is unable to do anything to save himself. Also, those that are unsaved are dead to themselves, to others and God. We need the intervention of Jesus Christ to be made alive, whereby the trinity of man will constitute the image and likeness of God. No one sees evil to be bad only the bad. What man does is spoken of as evil. I remember when I wanted to start doing the right thing. First I had to get away from evil namely the spirit of drugs and the influence of people doing wrong. I to had options. I could keep on shooting dope and in time kill myself or could accept Christ and allow the Holy Spirit to work on me on the inside. I chose the latter.

Thank God.

We tend to forget that we are spiritual being's now when we tend to usurp our will over God's. We are no more than Satan when we tell God that he didn't do this or he didn't do that, and what he didn't create now. When things of this nature come about well I'll say this, I don't think that it's right for the child to tell the parent that they are in control, especially when they are underage.

Some people have this despairing ability for selective reasoning that tells them that they don't need to pray. They don't need God, that it's all about them. But I want to bring to your attention that the devil knows God. I am but a man that's been reformed and refined by the word of God, and that I've formed a relationship with his son and you need to do likewise. But then that's on you. It's really a need to trust Jesus if they are to keep our sanity and soundness of mind. This journey isn't easy but necessary concerning the disillusion of man that he is his keeper.

We need to look at the things that are happening around us. We need to understand that absolutely nothing happens to us, for us, around us, that don't affect us in one way or another. Be it good or bad. The bondage of whatever must be overcome by you no matter what befalls your affections with the unseen must be overcome with the seen. We must overcome this sickness and know the one that can help us navigate this sea of uncertainty. Brothers and sisters, we need to listen to the masterful events of this perplexed society and know that it won't be long. People that run from anything will never be close to nothing. Every creature on earth should realize that there's no animals greater than them except man.

Man has a spirit about him that keeps him in disarray about himself, and his total being is fighting against itself. Now, most of the time all we need is a trigger and that trigger can be all most anything that he or she fancies, or intoxicates them to the point that they need something more that themselves to feel normal. Anything or anybody that need something to feel normal is addicted to the same and that's as real as it gets.

Lord, help me. I need for you to help me with this madness that has contaminated my life by the unrelenting pressures of this world. Father, I want to know you as my Lord and savior. I need to have a daily commune with you and your father. I need for you to help me with this madness that has consumed my life and stolen the ambition from me to amend my life that was derailed on false promises. I became weak to the things that would keep me and others from your love, grace, and mercy. But father I've come to my senses and I want to accept your Son as my savior. So Lord Jesus come into my life, save me from myself. I need a relationship with you. So help me. I am tired of running. I thank you in the name of Jesus.

Being saved is a wonderful thing when you make up your mind to do so, and when it takes place you become interested in anything and everything we need. Just like when we were small, in the natural state, we need someone to help us learn this new and exciting way of living that we have accepted. This is such a wonderful and clean way of living and you will enjoy it. So much that there really won't be time for you to think about the foolish things that you did in the past. I know I didn't. Unless I am asked to compare the two or I am bearing witness to someone.

Father,

Help the babies to stay with you. Give them great grace and boldness to do your will. Send angels to help them with the negative things that will be said and done to them. Father, in the name of Jesus, give them the will to do your will. Help them to overcome the foolishness of this world so they can stand in the marvelous light of Jesus Christ. I thank you in the name of Jesus to give us great grace.

When we stand on the word of God there will be a renewed confidence in us, for us, towards us. People respect you and your God especially if they have seen and heard your trials that inflate one's ego, and build to the point that his faith is renewed in God and man.

Everybody wants and need someone in their life to be liked or to idolize, and this sometimes will get you into a heap of trouble. We

THE BEGINNING... THE END... ANEW!

sometimes latch on to things that are not good to us as well as no good for us. I am not saying that we seek out the bad things but sometimes I wonder there's no need to answer. I know already. I am about to tell you the bad choices that was made for me because I wanted to be good with everybody. This will happen to you when you think there is no hope of finding your way out of the hell that was chosen for you. All through your life you have become leery of everything and everybody, and after a while we become comatose to the thing's in play and become conformed to the ways of a raging fire of selfishness. Now, most of us live in a fantasy world, daydreaming about the whimsical far-fetched desire of the way we think that God is or is not as for me and my house.

My name is Zedart Hodges, Jr. I am the hostage that's been pinned hoping that there may, by chance, be someone who has come to them self or a right way of thinking, just long enough to make up in your mind to do the right thing.

The people that I've written about are real although dead or imprisoned. This is a true indicator of one's journey in life with and without the positive members in your life to relate to.

First of all, there was Mike, we grew up around the corner from each other. He went off to war and came back with the knowledge of drugs. When he got back he was turned out, and we were alright, so he turned me out.

Then there was the place we used to hangout and beat up people especially on payday. Along with this guy named John Dave, we were feared on this end of town we grew up on.

My family used to live over a pool hall that had a store this place called Clark's Corner. That's where we grew up, I was introduced to white whiskey plus there was a lot of liquor houses on that end of town. Also, there was only one place to work called J.P Taylor and everybody at some point in time worked there.

Then there was this first guy I had seen that had died of drugs. This draws my interest because I was told that there were no drugs around. Drugs had given me the best high so I started looking.

For a few years I hung around this pool room on the other side of town on James street, this was the place every hustler in town and even some from out of town. All you needed to do was wait. Also from time to time we shoot a game of pool or two and try to hook up with somebody that had some drugs so you wouldn't get sick until found a supplier.

After I found one I would make arrangements to have drugs delivered to my house. Curl Service if you will, I had that kind of relationship with most pushers. Then there was this guy that put the n in nasty. This dude didn't care about nothing of nobody. He had two down falls, one he was bout crazy, and two, this guy love to gamble. I remember when we would go boosting we would go to this gambling house to sell our goods. In this house money would be stacked on the table and sometimes they would be playing lowball or Georgia skin. To be strung out on drug's is a dangerous thing. I look back and all I can do is thank God I was given water shoots and everything. Jesus, thank you for saving me.

Come on let's talk to the Lord. Come on let's do this. Say;

Father,

I know that this is a wicked world because I've been touched by some of its wickedness with my use of drugs. I know that it's wrong but I am weak, I am not strong in my body or spirit. Lord I need help. Father, I am asking you to give me the strength and will to

THE BEGINNING... THE END... ANEW!

do your will. Father, I need for you to be in my life. I want to know your love to feel your presence in my life. Lord, I thank you, I praise your name, I give your presence glory in my life and ask you to strengthen me and help me to overcome this foolishness in my life. Only your word can satisfy the mysterious and baffling subject of life and death. Father I want to live to thank you in Jesus name.

I remember this other friend of mine named Monkey. He would say, let's go get paid or go boosting. This was nothing for us since we did this like it was a job. Also there was only a crew of three of us at the most 4 four. We would creep to boost or steal, or do anything that would get us to our goal of that dollar bill. The level of our success would depend on an array of things in most of the shams. The drama plays a huge part, that you ever thought about drug addiction, you know a person on drugs can go into any city and within a few minutes can locate where the spots are.

Remember I told you in the past there's only a few OD's left. I wasn't lying, most are still lost and really don't want to be found. But this O.D that I told you about that wouldn't give you eye water to cry. Well, he died with cancer but even though he was nice and nasty, he accepted Christ. Before that time came that's about the only good thing that I remember he did. Then there was this other guy, his name was Frank. This brother was the guy alone with this other brother named Lamont, what an almost crazy guy.

This brother would have no one but two valves of dope already fixed, one was filled with cocaine and the other would be filled with horse which would be called speed balling. Then I tried this, man this was high then, later on, there were crack and heroin. Now this high was a high that would take you higher as high as you wanted. To go high that high, one must know, as someone once said, man has got to know his or her limitations. There has to be times in one's life when you know in your heart that if I do this much dope, I'll die. But then there was a lot of times when I didn't care. But most of the times when you fix up your drugs you can just about to say this is too much. I was greedy but I was mindful, does that make sense? Maybe not to you. But to someone out there that's cautious because nobody really wanted to die being a drug addict of any sort is really about rebellion. But that rebellion's hard to get away from once it takes hold don't you agree. I know you do love yourself is the beginning of freedom, but as I said before, freedom isn't free.

Then there was this other brother name Tyron this young man somehow did something with some drugs and his hole arm just withered up to the point where it was just there. So he was like a one-arm man. He had to do everything with his left arm, you say that's nothing but he was right-handed.

Life is so good but you can only realize this fact if you are tired of this way of tricking yourself with the idea that you know it all, or that it owed you something. How we were only promised seventy years and even, that depends on your hatred for sin in your life. You know, a lot of time I will be talking to people and they would say I don't believe in Jesus. But when you believe or don't believe in Jesus, the bible says you don't believe in God now most people only repeat what they hear. If you hear wrong you speak wrong, if you don't think that you are worth saving you will never begin the process of saving yourself, and if you don't think you are worth it, you will always believe that people are against everything is against you.

But that's not the cure for your whole being. This is acted upon or is driven by the need for drugs or some type depending on your drug of choice.

Then there was this girl or lady from K-town, and she had this friend name Donnell that knew the note game. Like I said before,

THE BEGINNING... THE END... ANEW!

everybody has something they were pretty good at. Only some knew most of the games. Drugs seem only the boost you to think that's good for them.

When you are in the game you tend to lump shoulders with a lot of folks including cops that are not so clean. Lawyers and all, well what I am about to say will seem to straight forward but it's real, and it's the only way that real change will come about in a life that you desire.

You know, drugs have robbed our communities for so long. They have made us lose our perspective of life and its meaning. Disconnected families to the point that we kill each other mercilessly. They are bad for us and our people. Like I always say, it isn't any fun when the rabbit got the gun.

There are numerous ways to not hear what's good for you when you are bent on doing wrong. You can always walk away, ignore the person, change the conversation. But we must never break the line of communication because everybody has something to say to you good or bad, and it be up to you to decide whether or not to listen. No matter how we feel, we must never break the connection with the Creator no matter the reason, or you will begin to slip downhill, trust me.

Now, the Bible tells us that we were, in the beginning, predestined by God. But when you be talking to someone, they say it was meant to be. When we do foolish things I don't think that this was meant to be, the God I serve is about righteousness, not the wrongness.

Let us make sense of the issue here. You live on a block were someone is always hatting on you but they don't know that there this other guy that has your back. No matter what, the other guy is always trying to trick you. Nut no matter what the trick, all you need to do is ask for help and you get it no matter physical or mental.

Also when you ask for help there's nothing that this other guy won't do for you. Even if you think that you have enough strength. That's when he will help you more, all you need to do is ask for his help. But pride keeps them from help, one really need to help themselves. Now, the dope game isn't for the weak, you got to know that an addict of any status is a badass. Anytime one put something in their mouth or arm, not knowing that effects other than it will make you high. Well you must be willing to fight first for your spirit then your soul and lastly your body in that order. Anything other than that won't work. Now I know that a lot of folks would say that they can handle things. But you need to stop lying yourself.

PART 3

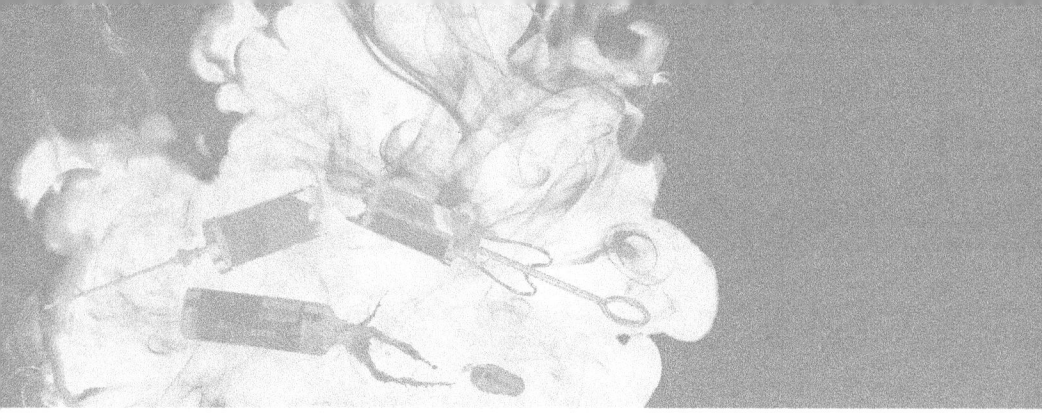

There are a lot of people in my life that I must thank. Those that know me as well as them that knew. Most of all, to the keeper of my soul for when I was out there strung out like a research monkey wanting to stop but couldn't find the strength to begin the process. Now my desire was to be clean. This is what I really wanted. I kept being introduced to God but was still missing the mark. People will tell you that you need to know God, but then they don't tell you that it's mandatory also that we form a relationship with Jesus. I thank God that I was introduced to his son. It was only then that my dreams of being clean started to manifest in my life. The desire was not there before to even start the journey to freedom.

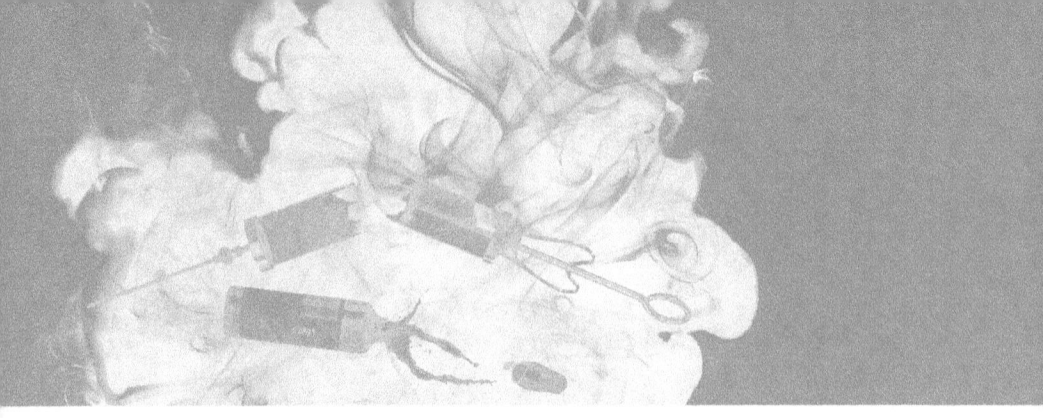

THANK YOU, LORD.

T̲hank you for helping me to see that we have power over the enemy. But only through you will this power be manifested in my life. Lord, I know now that I need to be strengthened by you. So I make you Lord of my life to begin this walk by faith of freedom. To know you will for my life and also to understand what I must do for my fellow man. Thank you for helping me see past the forest. Thank you for helping me to see that things that I did was not normal. thank you for being my keeper in Jesus name. Amen

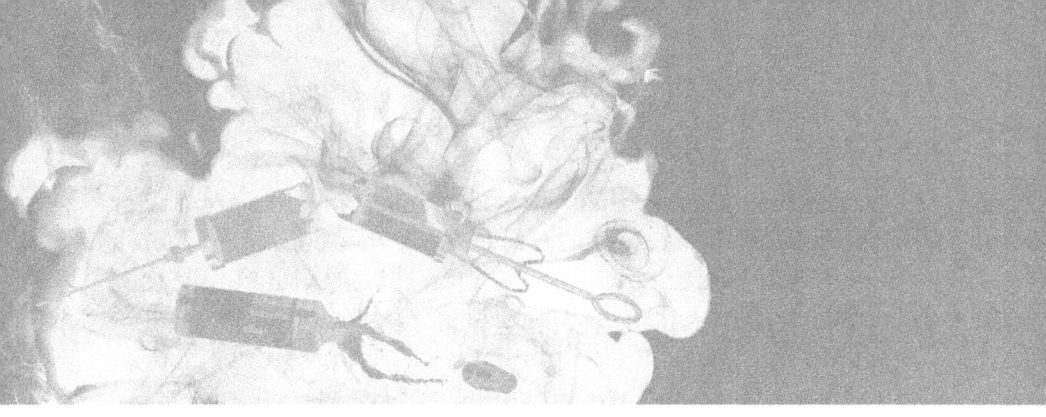

CONVERSATIONS

This title was aided on my heart early on and as I started to reach its end I thought it more and more fitting as I was reaching its end. This title made sense because I will be talking about everything. Maybe not as in depth as a lot of folks would like but maybe enough so that one would go to church or study the Bible or go Sunday school. If they are not scared and inquire about things they don't understand, get it from the horse's mouth. So to speak this Christian life is one beggar asking another where did he get that bread that seem to keep him filled.

There's this atmosphere of unbelief that is running rampant in this world. In your state, in your community, hell even in your home. Listen to your state because some people think that it's okay to go against the power that is community. Because thinking is contagious moreover bad thinking is deadly, a lot of folks may not believe this but sin will draw you. Now, a lot of people believe in the existence of God but not his power. So they have a form of freedom but they are intellectually in denial when it comes to communion with Jesus Christ. Let me speak a little knowledge to you which you may or may not know or just don't want to believe. God is a spirit, his perfect in knowledge, holiness, righteousness, and faithfulness, and mercy. Some men think that as long as they don't let their kids see them do something wrong like arguing or fighting. The right thing as far as family is they don't go to church but let their kids see them do the right thing. With family, they would say they know God but they only have that household religion and one would think that because they are the man of the house. They don't want their kids to see them on their knees asking for help, which is a hard thing when you don't know how to explain God to them. Then they start talking to outside images that more than likely, will tell them that they don't need to do this, they don't need to do that, and the next thing you know here comes Johnny Law, and you wonder why.

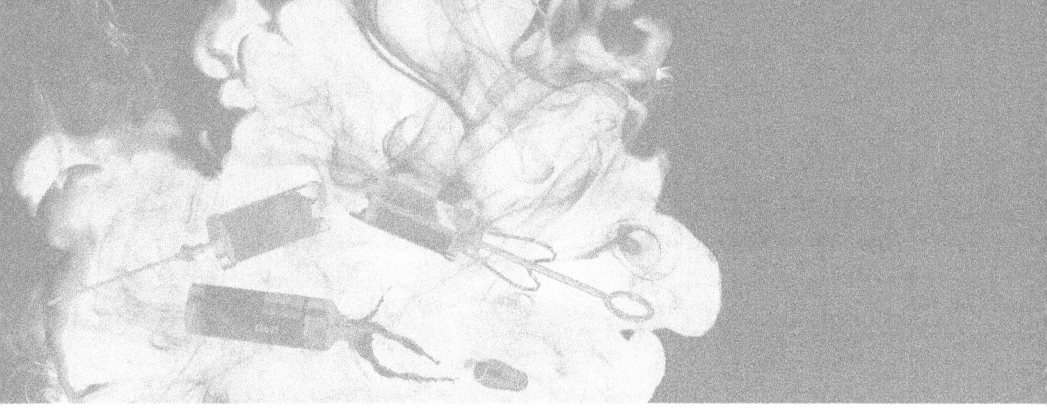

LOOK AT THIS

YOU KNOW A LOT ABOUT now but not enough about then. Don't get it twisted, we are always to remember the dry times in our lives

But we must also know that we need help to stay away from the drawing power of evil because sin comes in and out of itself will draw you back in, and make it more and more impossible to comprehend. The meaning of your life as previously assigned to you by the Doctor. Now, as for some folks they would say there are many paths to God which may or may not be favorable, depending on the person or persons in question. Many paths but only one door.

We all have our differences and there are plenty of dislikes around but in the end we will meet spiritually at the same place. Also we must realize that it's our soul that's in question. Our spirit goes back to God our body back to the earth. But our soul this is what's in question and according to God's word, we will be made aware of what's going on.

Now a lot of folk's use drugs or whatever as whole hearted excuse to not look for themselves in God. Most folks won't allow themselves to even attempt to have a conversation about the Creator but when they get sidelined with the irritating affairs of the police or sheriff department, then they call God. But God says, I am not trying to hear you unless you recognize my son as Lord of your wayward life. I created you to worship my son and thank me for not allowing Satan to take you out when you overdosed off of on pills, dope, or whatever. Since you don't think it's worthwhile to be knowledgeable of me and my son, I'll give you over to a depraved mind. To do what you think is good for you. But remember it's a fearful thing to fall into the hands of the living God.

I know that you are probably saying why are you telling me all this. I say I know you. I've been where you are and it took me a few minutes but we got it done. So I am free from the ill-founded ways of an addict that's unwanted by society. Sidetracked by his so-called friends and alienated by all that drug game isn't no joke. Nothing changed the picture, is still the same. So you see, I know you even thought we've never meet. That's just something I thought I would throw out there.

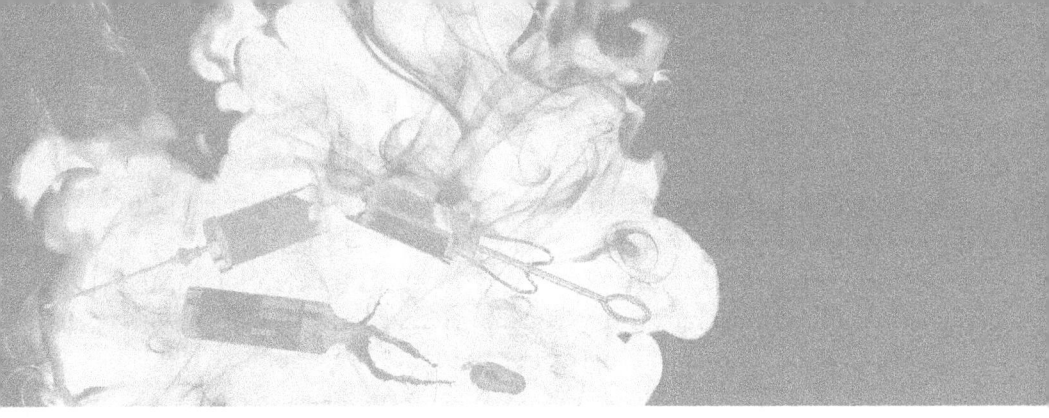

REMEMBER

>Only one creates all others destroys
>Only one adds all others subtracts
>Only one love's all other's gate
>So which one do you want in your life?
>Show me.

Now you will start to think am I the only one going through this. Well it will seem just this way but I am here to let you know that people are pulling for you. They just don't know how, and yes, there will be some that don't even want to be in your presence. Even if they have or know the means by which help. You will help them or we can't be upset with them when we stole from them. There are folks that will never forgive. Those are the people that in their heart is hardened and there' no one to blame but self. There is one that can soften the hardest of hearts who is Lord of lords and King of kings. You know him to now.

When the time has lapsed on what you think is the end, it is only the beginning. If you are truly interested in finding yourself and understand that when you start this journey of renewal of your mind body and soul back to where you believe it supposed to be won't be easy. There's only good and bad. Now, even the good isn't good but the bad isn't better, it's the way you allowed situations to play out. Especially when you didn't want to be held accountable to anything other than what we gave most of our attention to, and this will be most harmful to you and yours no matter who or what this maybe. I am speaking from experience don't get it twisted.

Furthermore, when we, by this I mean Christians as a group or an individual begin to talk to someone, anyone that doesn't want to make a commitment one way or the other they will say oh I am very spiritual so let's not go there. The Devil is also spiritual. Look the word of God that says if you have, not the spirit of Christ, you are none of his body as God's creation.

I know that most of us think that freedom means to be free and it does. Let's be clear if freedom is to be adhered to in our lives, there must be a sacrifice made at some point.

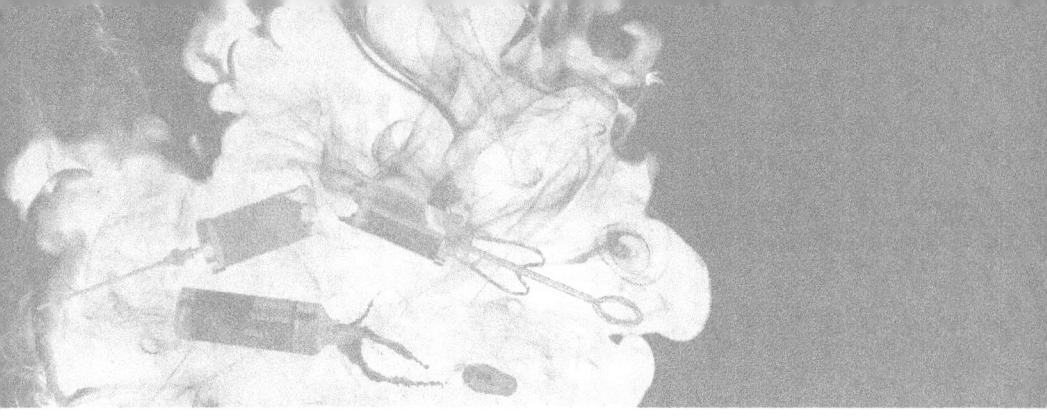

FREEDOM

LIBERTY FROM SLAVERY EXEMPT FROM bondage. This world is hard at work trying hard to take us away from our roots. Our way of life and even from God and his son. But hold, on help is on the way. We need to be cleansed from the inside out. But in order for this to be accomplished we need God's help through Jesus Christ. Trust me, I know first-hand also through this venture that there is nothing more important than trust in yourself and faith in your fellow man. This life of drug madness can only be defeated through faith and trust.

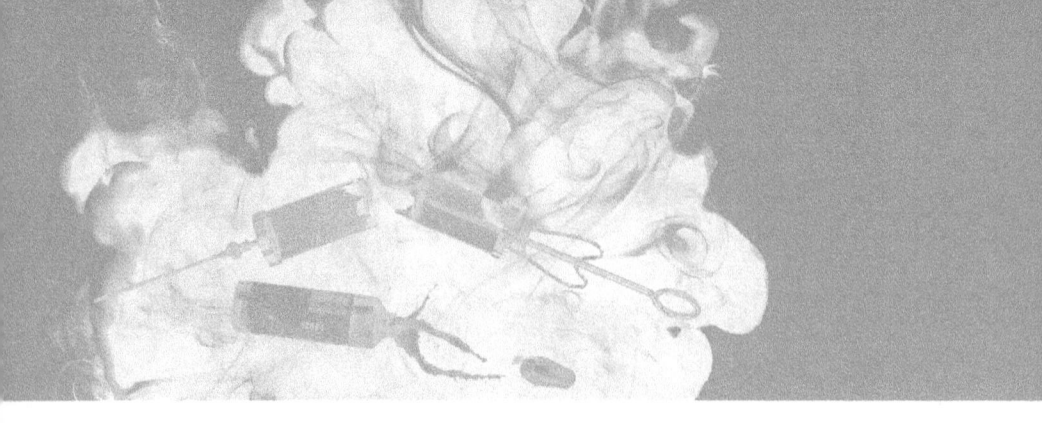

I AM NOT A SLAVE

Since the beginning, in one way or another, we are still enslaved by something or somebody.

If it sounds good we're in it to make it. We will do it if it makes any sense. We tend to get strong out on that particular product and more often than not, people will do whatever to stay in the mainstream. Also, when we begin to see the wrongness of what we think is right, it is usually too late and every chance Satan gets the stick to us. Because Satan fights the battle in our head. That's where the war is waged. All we need is to accept God and trust in Jesus Christ and acknowledge him as savior. Unless you know Jesus as your Lord and savior, you are short in spirit status and stature.

We can do this through Christ. Moreover, in our thinking become stubborn, remember we are always full of foolish thoughts. This is the action that will determine your level of sanity. Some folks are not crazy, they are just mean and think that because things don't go their way. They can do anything that they wanted and not pay attention to people's feeling, pushing back the knowledge of respect while grasping the adolescent notion that whatever you got is mine. They become a bully growing up and if anybody lost their position, an argument arises. Most of us only know one way to settle the affair because they were not trained up in the way they should go. A lot of times the parents are not trained, so what does that even say?

Life only shoots you a curve if you won't follow the rules or should I say the law of society. These days, no one plays fair and will sway most people to say and do anything possible. Especially the never-ending folly of our youth. To think what has happened to the person or nation's rife with perjury, extortion bribery, forgiveness, slander, also using profanity as if it's our national language.

We must each determine the value of God's word in our lives and affairs. God's law is and should be supreme. In one's life, God's law and word must never be altered or diluted. To mean less than what it means to the hearer. Now, if this does happen, remember God is not mocked. Every knee shall bow and every tongue shall confess that Jesus Christ is Lord.

To be ruled under pressure is unacceptable, but to be affirmed and know the love of God atones us. Through Jesus Christ you need to recognize everything that's damning to the wellbeing of a person or people of color. It can and will be hurdled at ones during their life especially if there is a defect in one's character. Also, in your journey to manhood or woman society as a whole will disown you or anyone that they think know or see that don't conform to their way of thinking and of living. I think and do believe that this is why God is in spirit, so no race, group, denomination or person has or think they have a monopoly on the Creator. I also believe that only through Christ can one have fellowship with God.

I can see why some people are fooled into believing in the power of the destroyer. The tormentor of the mind, the wicked one that put ideas in one's head. Look, this guy deceived the whole world so you know that you are no match when confronted by the satanic demons. Now, as an integral part of the power of darkness, the most interesting part of this madness is for one to know that the younger one is the more disobedient they become.

This is why we need to start early. The enemy moves in and constructs a thought pattern around one's sin or one's attitude. They will become more and more rebellious as time progresses. This is why we should train up a child in the way he or she should go look somebody well-trained. But you turned somewhere.

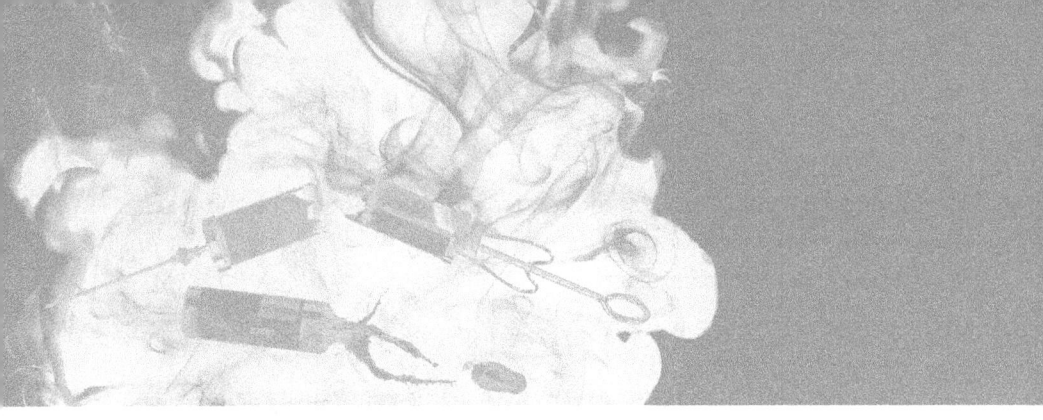

TRANSFORMING OUR MINDS

It won't be easy for a nobody that want to start over. We need the power of God through Jesus Christ. A lot of people will and do say I don't need anybody and that's true. Truth is we don't need somebody, all we need the spirit of God. When he gives us power over the enemy, the power to overcome anything that hinders us from becoming His treasured possession. We will have more power and knowledge for unmasking the enemy. Satan wants to interrupt your journey with God, interfere with your dreams and attack your well-being.

Unfortunately, most of the Western world has rejected the idea of a supernatural evil. There is a large blind spot when it comes to the spiral side of man. We need to have a healthy recognition and knowledge of our enemy as well as our own identity. Everybody should trust in God, but when it comes to trusting in the Lord and Jesus Christ, you have to take your time and think about this for a very short bit. The very essence of sin is to choose our will rather than God's will. Here's the real deal, if you tolerate a little sin then more sins will follow.

Don't be scared or as someone from the right side of the track's would say, don't be afraid. Be that as it may we must not be champs when it comes to serving God.

My main objective early on was to shoot as much dope as I could. As we went from town to town stealing everything that wasn't nailed down. We would steal the night deposits from bank's country stores. We would do almost anything to get high. I used to shoot dope on the church steps, riding down the highway at 70-75 miles an hour. Trusting that while I was driving my partner would be shooting dope on my arm or neck, depending on where I could find a vein. This was our spiteful payment to ourselves for not getting caught after stealing all day. I say spiteful because we thought that the world owed us something. Nothing can be more further from the truth.

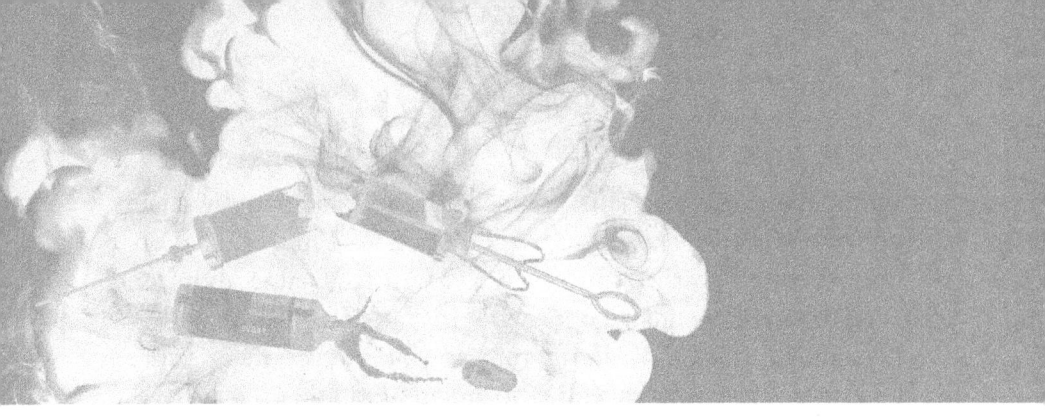

THE PLIGHT DEEPENS

B LACK MAN AROUND THE WORLD and especially in the United States is portrayed by far as the most part, a lack of education. As well as staggering unemployment statistics, has brought us and people of color. Although the problems afflict poor black men as have been known for decades, the new data paints a more extensive and sobering picture of the challenges they face.

We can no longer ignore the more sobering and scarier routine or the revolving doors that incarceration provides. One of the more commonplace stories that I can bear witness to.

Most people with any sense will admit to their own bad choices but say they also battle a pervasive sense of hopelessness. In response, the worsening situation for young black men on a growing number of programs is placing as much importance on teaching.

Life skills like the resolution of conflicts, character building, along with job skills and business savvy, these are a litany of problems facing young black men and woman, as well as people of color. From the inner-city neighborhood across this world notwithstanding if someone wants to change. Only from the inside out and not the outside in, and even then it depends on one's will to attain this goal.

Punishment and inequality in one's self brought about by society will throw one back into active addiction. We must realize that only through spiritual intervention will this came about and even then, it depends on one's will. To stay to his nature with his personality, it is God's nature to keep you, but you must want to be kept. Christianity is really the only religion that sets forth the supreme being as love. Addiction demands love.

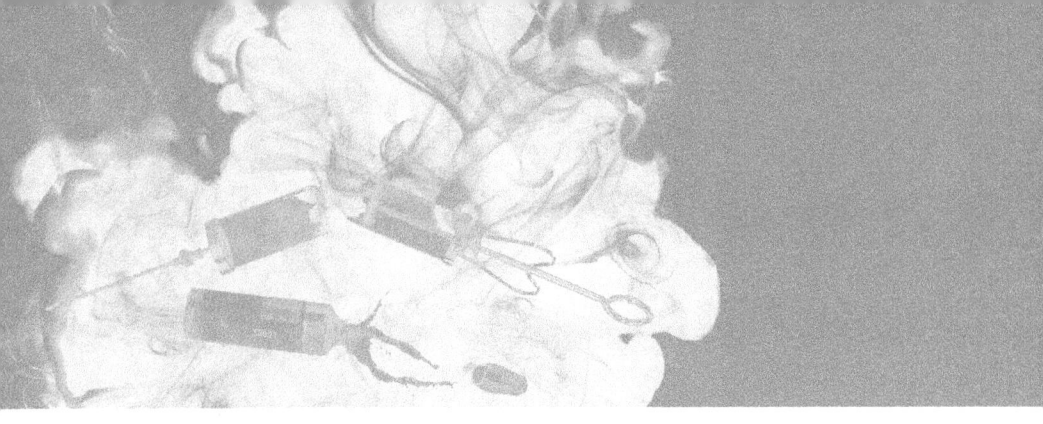

LET'S PRAY FOR THE FATHER

I'M ADDICTED TO THESE DRUGS and helpless in this battle beyond myself. Father, I want you to help me with this supernatural evil. Lord, I ask you to come into my life as savior and Lord. Father, Satan incites weakness and immorality. Lord, give me the strength to overcome this stage of self-destruction. Father, you said in your word that you are a keeper. Lord, keep me from myself I want to be kept from all dangers. Father, I thank you in the name of Jesus I give you honor praise and glory. In the name of Jesus Christ my Lord.

Writing this book understandably was very important to me as a lot of people won't even believe you unless someone has sobriety on their side. For some length of time I thank God for both. Also for everybody that's going through need to identify with someone of like mindedness. Too hooked on one's self and the exploration of life's encounter with death daily is a high all by itself. I'm here to tell you that demons are promoting Satan's agenda through people. They control through various means that we as believers cannot be demon-possessed, we can be demon influenced this about this. A spiritual program in some circles is unexpected

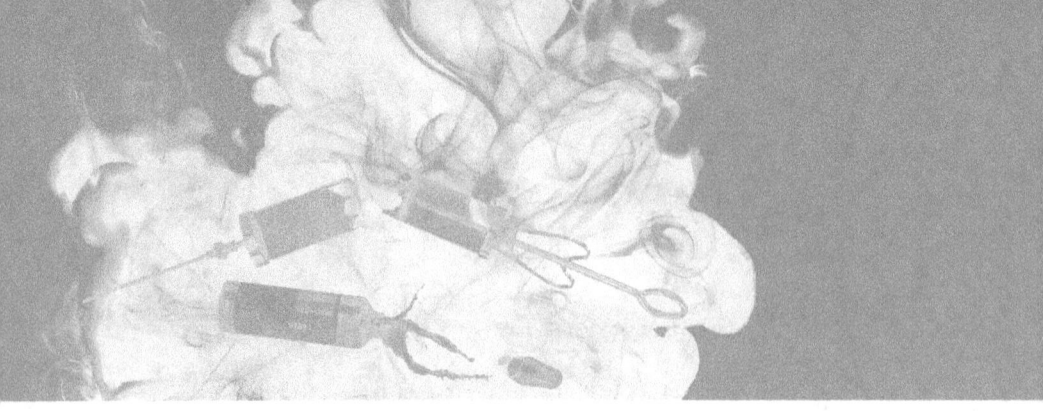

SPIRITUALITY IS A WAY OF LIFE

Security - the security of the believer is a theological expression based on scriptural revelations. Underlying the doctrine of assurance.

Life and death - only in the Bible can any satisfying light be found on the mysterious as well as baffling subjects of life and death.

Grace - is unmerited favor of God toward men.

Gospel - means good news or glad tidings.

Forgiveness - an eternal unchanging law of the universe.

Praise - is an expression of approval or admiration.

Inheritance - believers are heirs of God and joint heirs with Christ.

Peace - quiet, peacefulness, tranquility, restfulness, calm, we have peace with God from the moment of our salvation the peace of God is the experience of believers as they engage in prayer supplication and thanksgiving.

Also, just as he who called you is holy, you too should be entirely holy in your behavior. For the scripture say, be holy for I am holy. God can never compromise when it comes to his character.

The tears of humanity is only the tearing down of the walls of human inadequacy to overcome the will of human bondage.

There is an expectation of love, peace, redemption, stewardship and service. Along with joy and self-worth if one decides to conform to the will of God.

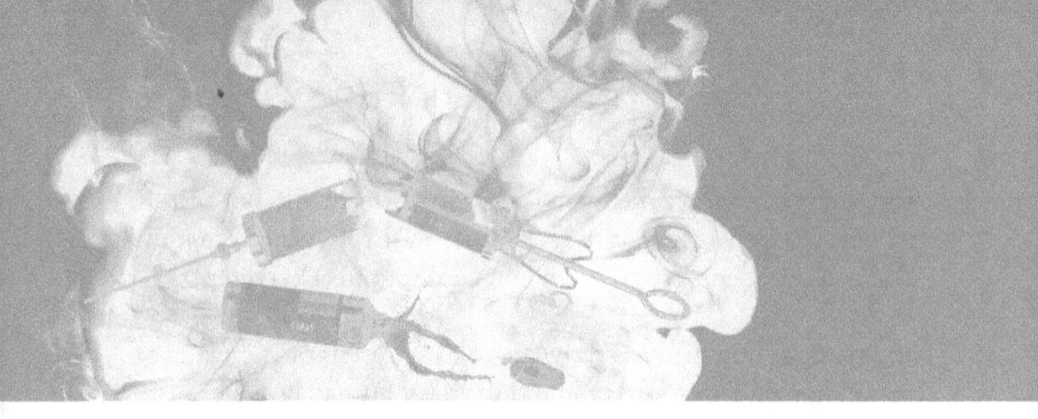

ABOUT THE AUTHOR

My name is Zedart Hodges, I'm married to Anne Jorge from Nairobi Kenya. I was raised in Goldsboro, North Carolina and growing up I was a bad boy. As a result I spent time in the correction system for the use and sale of drugs while in prison, I was introduced to this Jesus. At first I didn't think that he was real but over time I came to realize that without him nothing is possible.

After some time of shooting drugs and being caught in the revolving doors, I've come to know better. Trust me.

For a few years' now I've been perplexed by the fact that our young folk feel the need to flunk out at the class of life by upholding their want for drugs. Also, to be shackled and gripped with the realization that drugs need to be a lifetime venture which is untrue. Everybody be looking for something that they don't want to find even though there are various intoxicating notions of false reasoning on your part. Father forgive them for they don't know what they're doing. I invite you to revisit your own unhealed wounded past.

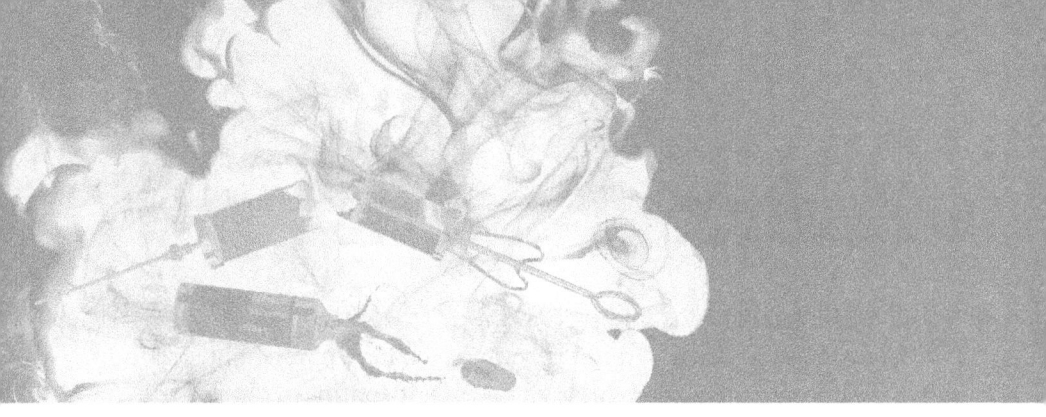

THE ATTACK ON THE MIND

We live in a corrupt world where most of us are governed by reprobate minds. Also, there are many people in position of authority that only think carnally. Our nation knows a lot about rights but not much about responsibility that was promised beforehand. It seems like when the time comes to be relocated, and they get in place it's not soon after that the lackey attitude and adopt the spirit of compromise there are people that's anointed but untrained and there's those that don't want to be trained for anything

But they value reputation over reality. Freedom is a source of joy. People who have been set free from the enemy's stronghold experience an amazing awakening to the spiritual side of self-awareness. Also in Christ, we will rediscover every aspect of our life from a victory perspective.

Where the spirit of the Lord is, a declaration of freedom, the supply of freedom is here. But something is cutting the line. Some people are codependent that is they are slaves to somebody or something, they are playing God in their lives. God can't be God in your life and is God isn't God in your life. There is no spirit control, there is a lot of confusion about freedom but God is not confused about where the dynamics of freedom is located. It comes to us through the spirit by faith.

True freedom means abiding how God's freedom apply to us today. If you are not spiritually free, it is because you have never embraced the gospel or because as a Christian you're not continuing in the truth. Notice also where true freedom is, it is found in truth. Just going to church is not enough to warrant freedom, we must allow our minds to be unlocked by the spirit of God. This was the problem with people all through Jesus ministry, no one believed it was for freedom that Christ died for us all. We must not be subject to the yoke of slavery again. the antidote for bondage, as well as slavery, must be nullified.

Somebody prayed for me. All of the time your mom or your grand mom is always lifting you or somebody, that's love. That's why I believe that some folks can do crazy things and don't anything happen. They may go to jail but nothing really bad happened. They may pray and God will hear your mom's pray or whoever and the Lord will give his angels charge over you. For man's sake, God will say listen young man or young lady, my Spirit will not always be proud to restrain sin, you had better take the clue. Have you ever wondered about why people die from the simplest things. Think about this.

Is he upset with me? This is a weightier matter than displeasure at sin. It's about his love or the wrath of God.

There is no gray area with God, it's either white or black, right or wrong, and it's always about his will for your life. He wants the best for you and yours. God's wrath against sin arises by necessity because of the justice of his law and the righteousness of his character.

God's wrath comes when his patience is ignored. We as God's creation can find no way around it. Nowhere to run from it and

THE BEGINNING... THE END... ANEW!

there is no distinction between big or small, black or white. Sin has no color, no degree. For nobody to say, this is more than the other you could be living in. Sin for two days or 20 years makes no difference. There is no repercussions for this and any actions.

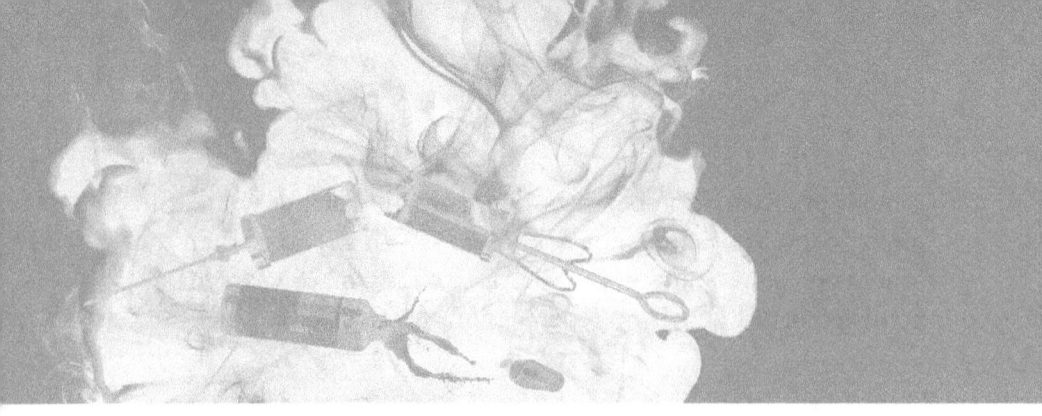

GOD'S LOVE

CHRISTIANITY IS THE ONLY RELIGION that sets forth the supreme being as love. Love is the expression of his personality corresponding to his nature. It is the nature of God to love beyond everything. There must be the action of love, this is a must. You must learn to love yourself before you can love someone or something else. Love is passionately and righteously pursuing the wellbeing of others as well as self. Now you may think I don't have or I am not capable of this much love. Well, borrow some from the Lord, there is power in unity.

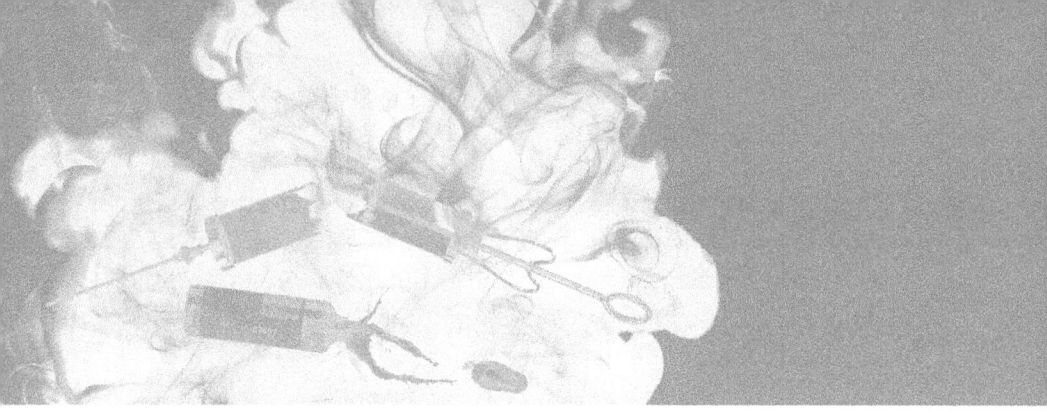

CLOSING REMARKS

One may say you have to stay in church too long and I will answer how long do you stay in the clubs. Another would say but you have to dress up and I will answerZ the Lord said to come as you are physically and mentally. This is a heart matter. She may say, but I don't have a baby sitter and I would say bring them to now.

A lot of people would say, but I don't feel like it and the Lord would say I didn't either.

Father take this cup nevertheless not my will but thy will.

We are members of God's household. His children whom Christ purchased with his blood. This should motivate a person to do the right in or out of church. Speaking of a church, there is no other organization except the church which has been called into being. By God Himself through the supernatural ministry of the Holy Spirit which has the specific task of carrying out Christ's work here on earth.

Father, help us with our unbelief. Give us the strength to stand against the evil one for we need help to navigate these waters of uncertainty. Come into my life and I'll make you my Lord and Savior. Thank you for what you've done and I praise you for what you're going to do in Jesus name. Amen.

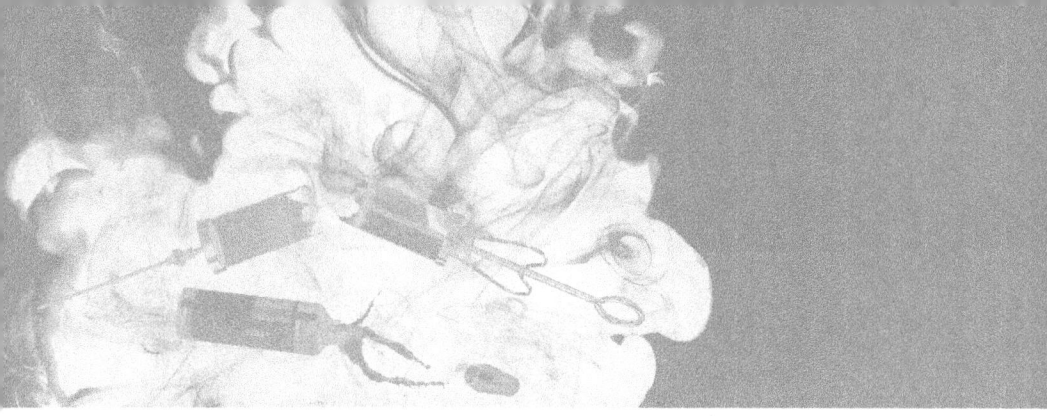

SECURITY

YOU KNOW MOST OF US won't do this or that because of insecurity. They are insecure about nothing in particular, it's just that their self-esteem is not their strong point. In time it comes. Now, this security is a very important component of salvation also it's one benefit of the spirit's presence in one's life. You may ask how do I get this internal sense of security? The spirit of the Lord only will assure one of this event.

The Bible is not asking you to forget your fleshly desires. But it is asking you to bring them under subjection. Now, the only way to stop walking in the flesh is to start walking in the spirit. It's true that you may be able to make a few minor improvements along the way. The authority, however, doesn't come from you. It comes from the authority of the Holy Spirit in you.

PART 4

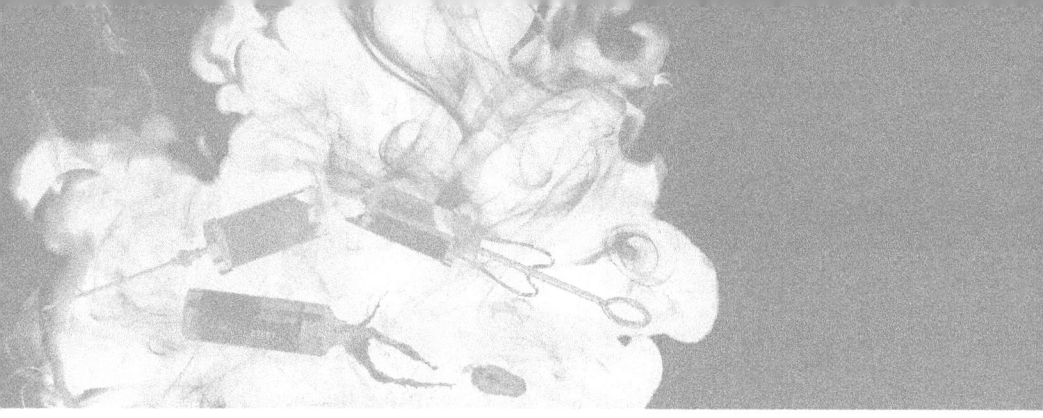

Are you aware of the men behind the star or badge? A few years ago it seemed as though war was declared on our youth. They are falling at the hands of those we have entrusted our safety with our very lives and as we look at the reason, most give a reason that Ray Charles can see through the thousands of our young people. Behind bars with nothing to look forward to, but a life of being ordered about like a herd of chickens being put in or loaded on trucks. To go to the death house and if we are not being hurled up, we are being outright shot down like seal pups. Before being aware that life is all that, when we kind of negate or nullify the inflated notion that life owes us something, that we didn't work it.

Now, understand that everything that we do has been done before. Where you are, I've been also. With where I am you must try to get there. Look mayhem has plagued our life from the beginning with mistrust. The strategy of defeat from family, friends, wife, husbands, and acquaintance alike. So we as black people, along with those that don't have as much money as others. Also, we understand that as well as the police killing us. We also kill except in killing, often times we don't look back. Usually it's a group thing so we are killing ourselves as well. Being shoot by the police with little or no worry on their part is amazing don't you think. For I know the thoughts that I think towards you, thoughts of peace and not evil. To give you a future and hope that blows me away even when you aren't thinking about him.

Since the beginning, hostile powers has reigned over man. From the start this reign has its origin in sin. The purpose of this punishment that God allows is only to those that oppose his will and purpose for their life to resist is futile.

No matter what we as a people do to salvage our position with humanity. Most people position with injustice is that this world or this city or this town belong to them. Look, you don't own anything not even the house you dwell in. So you think you do. There is something called Eminent Domain. They can just take your house or land and isn't nothing we can do. There is really nothing we can do to understand what God has in store for us unless we become friend with Jesus, and accept him and his teaching. You and everybody knows that this is God's domain, everything you can see along with that you can't.

Now this is his, and them that don't believe can conform. God will allow the death angel with permission to ride you like Roy Roger's road trigger. It is said that the more things change the more they stay the same.

Change in oneself is only afforded to us by acknowledging the fact that the acquisitions of life and living is only amazing to us. If one set goals that he knows that he will never reach with, our help from the creator. When we happen to reach the apex of the goal in question that we set for our self, we fail with our arrogant sense of superiority. Be still and know that I am God. This is what God almighty says.

Now that I am here, there is no God besides me. I was put to death and I bring to life. I have been wounded and I will heal and no

THE BEGINNING... THE END... ANEW!

men can deliver out of my hand. I am the baddest somebody you will ever know. I am God you may say, God won't do this, God won't do that and I say, read the book and believe.

People of old like the Abrahams, the Jacobs, the Elijahs, the Enochs, the Isaac, all them. What you might say were saved on credit. God overlooked their sins until Christ came and made payment. Keep in mind that perfection is what God accepts and we are only perfect through Christ if we believe only he can forgive and credit you with the perfection we need. Only he is qualified to bring people to God.

We must not form our opinion of God from the bottom up. We need to humble ourselves, study his word and works and ask humbly be built from the top down. There are horrendous injustices that exist on this planet for people of color. We must trust our God through Jesus Christ.

At any moment at any time our young folk maybe shot in the back, in the front, anywhere it doesn't matter. They are so horrific they challenge the very foundation of trust hope and faith. Our trust in the pope, our hope in the system and out of fear our faith in each other. Never shall I forget the flames which consume our faith in humanity. Why don't you know my friend? I am on a journey and I hope you will join me. Like all of us I face the danger of idolatry every day. That temptation to manufacture a God based on my inclinations and experience.

There are a great number of people that over time has gone from rags to riches. Some that are still around and some, of course, that has gone on somewhere I couldn't begin to know where up or down.

For every victory there is a problem, for every achievement there is a price. And Lord have mercy for every triumph. There must be a sacrifice, this is the law of the land instituted by God to bring his creation back to him through his son. Interestingly, with a lot of folks, genuine outward appearances mean nothing. Their IQs or how well they perform make no difference to us. None of that matters.

What matters most are the remarkable qualities that made them effective in life serving Christ.

The secret of survival is what you do ahead of time. In calmer waters parents spend time in God's word. Also, study the inspired charts he has given you for the journey of life deepens your walk with him through prayer and personal worship. Now, kids do what they see their life, they also will embarrass you whether you are around or not good at some time. They will say I am not going to church, my mom didn't. For your kids, you are the anchor for them. Reality say's it's part of throwing the anchor of reality and trusting God to bring you to shore.

You know there are so many things happening now that people gets to know that only the Messiah himself. For he knew of the coming of you and the breathtaking oppositions that would undoubtedly form the shell that you see as you look in the mirror. What's sad about looking back, it is sad to see and hear of the murders done by those we elect to protect and serve. It looks like the powers that he has declared war on people of color and as long as they get to decide that we got a lot of him or them to go. Remember Rodney, no more pretending. Instead journey with me back through time when cops learned how to beat people. People be taking movies and still this takes place. How much did you say a picture's worth really?

Everybody talks about how they love America but they be trying to disturb the progress of living. They waste time talking about

THE BEGINNING... THE END... ANEW!

nothing and if someone go through the procedures right. Just because you don't like them as a person, some people just lose it right or wrong. They can't be opening by dissuading someone. They disrupt everything even the wellbeing of an entire country. Now that's hatred on a grand scale. If people see the hatred of those in control, what do you expect from others that's not so in control of anything. A tender heart and a tough hide, that is the ticket. It's not an easy balance to maintain especially when you try to keep a refugee from a country being torn apart from within. The mistrust focused on one man I find no less in my study of life. I've noticed a pattern with heroes that men and women who stand tall and refuse to shrink. There exist on outside entity that helps them weather the storm in honor of their courage. Divine protection kicked in and I do believe because of their uninhibited faith in the Lord, we can stand tall.

I just can't seem to get away from this illegitimate action by the police that they call it mistake. Shootings sends their trigger happy ass across the way. You know, most of us don't even know what we are angry about. A lot of us just get mad because of the next person being mad. You're all are sure you want to handle this mad world on your own. We got cops shooting or killings, wars, we have the same-sex marriage, we have people stealing babies, folks killing on school campus. Now the Holy Spirit restraint will not allow sin to run rampant.

Throughout these conversations there are many things I neglect to talk about. But I think that respect is a worthwhile subject. We as a people are to give respect to our older people. Our wife or husband or kids and everybody that respect you and yours. But the problem is nobody know what this means any more. Nobody respects anybody, not even mom, dad, God. People say, I don't respect me some men yet he allows you to live. Respect don't mean any more. Everybody want respect but they don't want to give. They don't know what you need to get, people think that something is free to look. Isn't anything free? Not even water. Think about this please.

I want you to listen to my brothers and sisters. Life is so important. Now, especially since I Accepted Jesus as my friend. When you've grown up in the hood without any prominent male figure to give that definite form of expression that was established in your soul. That was a basic part of the gift that you inherited from God which some try to alter. and make people think that this is the way it supposed to be amazing. Therefore, we look at the opened scroll of human struggle and we embrace the lifestyle of victory and forget the misconceptions of being a victim. No one could open the scroll of human bondage. Now, the unopened scroll in your life speaks of human inadequacy. We need to chisel away at the wall of emotions that surround our heart.

The price of redemption is written on the inside of the scroll. When we were out there running up and down, the highways shooting dope. In and out of stores stealing everything that wasn't in a cage. It was fun at that time but as I get older I realized that this wasn't. What I was not made up to do this and when I begin to start loving myself and thanking God for not letting me O.D. or get shoot when I was creeping behind the counter of that country stores. I have been, as well as my people have been doped for so long that the elite of the community didn't really know how to communicate with us. Because of the commitment we had to drugs which had our undisposed ability to stay away from.

Doing dope isn't so bad until you find that when you don't have it. That you don't function any kind of way normal, you don't eat, think to speak in a rationalize way, all actions become questionable. Your skin becomes clammy cold to touch and it won't return to normal until getting a hit of whatever floats your boat.

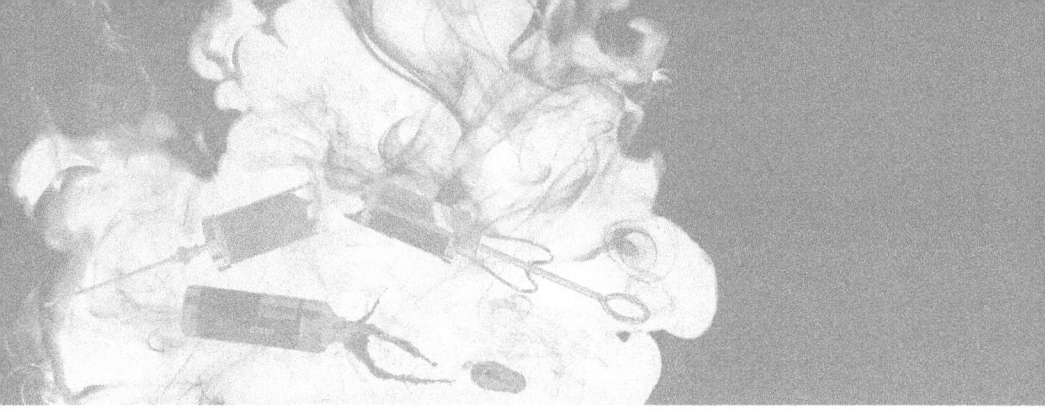

THE TEN COMMANDMENT PARAPHRASE

I AM THE ONE THAT HELPED you kick the habit when you were strung out like a research monkey.

I don't want you to smoke or do drugs or anything that kept you away from me.

I don't want you to be worshipping no bird, dog, cat, cow, snake, or no kind of animal other than anything than God. God is a jealous God.

If you hate me, I will make sure your children, your grand and your great grandchildren will catch all kinds of hell. But if you love me I'll show kindness.

Remember to keep the Sunday Sabbath day and keep it holy.

Don't be thoughtless with my name by cursing and all that.

Rest on the seventh day. Go to church.

Don't steal.

Don't lie.

You must not want to take anything that belong to your neighbor.

These are a few things that I wanted to paraphrase for you. One reason why I think that a lot of folks retract or drawback is that the preacher doesn't really know that he or she can go anywhere. With the word, I believe that as long as they stay on track at the beginning, during and especially at the end of the interpretation of the Book of Life.

People fail to realize that God controls the future. God controls everything. We need to say Lord allow your Lord to be in control of my life. Allow him to give to me the strength and wisdom through my Lord and Savior Jesus Christ whom you raised from the dead to preach salvation.

We need to let God, be God. This may sound cheap but often fall into the trap of trying to confine God to our perception of him. Again, one sign of this is the common malady of thinking or saying things like God would never allow that, wrong answer.

If this is a problem for you go to the lord in prayer, and give him permission to be Lord in your heart, and talk to him like you would talk to a close friend. Don't just say something and leave. Wait for him to speak.

We are to worship or ask him in spirit and truth but God has put in each of us to relate to him. Through the spirit we have in us we all possess, the image of God. That image with us includes at least an intellectual volition and emotion. It is with these elements of our personality that we are able to relate.

THE BEGINNING... THE END... ANEW!

I remember back in the early days when most of us in my town first started to do drugs and the cop wasn't really on top of what was going on. On hot days we were on the block and this pusher didn't have a lawn mower, this girl and me were sick so in a little while we saw this figure from way down the street walking. As the figure got closer and closer we saw that it was this lady. After this I knew that we would be alright, this was before they started to chain stuff together.

No matter where we are or what we are trying to do, if it's wrong, greed will prevail. At some point you may run into someone that will say that or you will believe they are fair. But somewhere when dealing with him or her, they will get over on you one way or another. It may be giving you a water shot, short change you or something, trust me. And everybody wants something for nothing. Even salvation, which is a gift from God, but there must be a sacrifice. You have got to give up something but understand the love of the Lord is the beginning of wisdom. And the knowledge of the Holy One is understanding. Also, God will show you how to live a wise life, a lot from us have book sense but no common sense. God will give the latter

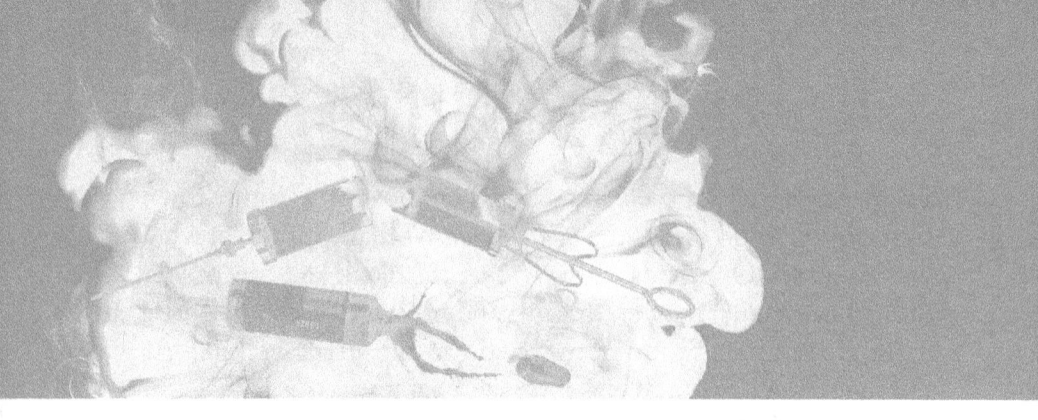

STAND FIRM

You know for a long time when I heard this phrase, I really was puzzled by it. Then one day I said, let me see what this stand firm mean. So I looked up both words and it mean to be stable and not be subject to change.

A lot of folks, when it comes to drugs of any kind, when they start feeling bad well, they throw their stand from out the window. What I didn't like is pain at first maybe. The second time I would say, I am about to take care of this problem because I hated pain. Now, when you need to stand firm, I found that the only way I could stand firm or hold on is to ask for help, to endure the pain. To do this, He will help but you must be willing to stand firm. Mean what you are saying and asking. For the Lord will help.

Chances are we as a people have so much to try and overcome. First we are blessed but we have the misfortune of being reared in less than admirable accommodations, and that is not our parents fault. I sure they did all they could but life will sometime throw you a curve. You can either catch it or hit it out of the park. And by hitting it out of the park, I mean, don't allow anything to get you off track. You need to stay focused on staying clean to keep

THE BEGINNING... THE END... ANEW!

your mind sharp. Respect others and trust in whoever you respect the most. For me, it's the Lord.

Now I can honestly say that the Lord was far from my mind when I was out there shooting drugs, stealing whatever chances are. If I had not met my friend, things would be different, I'm sure.

There is a young man I knew when I was out there. He was a good guy but he was a bank robber and he wrote a book and the title is, *Not Without Scars*. What a book. Have you ever wonder why someone that don't go to church always fear sometimes better than those that are called real Christian. What I mean by real Christian is, I mean, those that seem to be too good that they go to church, they don't raise a whole lot of hell, they are mindful of their parents, they are just good folks. Then there are those folks that God seem to always be doing crazy, and it seem that they always good. Things happen to or for them. Well somebody be praying for them or have prayed for them in the past. If this happen to someone you know, remember, God will not go against his promise that he made to your parents, grandparents, your auntie, or whoever. You got me, study the book.

I'm happy that I used to be drug addict, you can know at this moment. And I truly understand how important it is to rid yourself of this mellow madness that has robbed our communities and society at large. Now, the way one must get rid of this string of madness is to put your trust totally in the Creators hands. Also, you need to pray and ask God to take the desire, not the drugs, because they will always be desired. The more we do the more of what we want, but not this desire that is a want, and it is not necessary meaningful in one's life. Ask God to take the desire, not the drugs. You must be a fanatic about asking the Lord about removing this desire from your life. I thank you and praise your Holy name.

This Demonic Protocol has been released on humanity and fear is the vehicle. In this somewhat subnormal space of time, we should be looking toward the police for protection. Instead, they are intent on driving a wedge between police and public. We know that there is a three-three strike law and after a while, things will start to look real bad. Whoever they want to lock up they will be able to use this three-strike law no matter what the third stake is. You have seen a bad boy now, Satan is about generation bashing as well as an individual discomfort for living and life. Most of the people that's been shot were in their early twenties or someone that our teens.

One could look to and talk to and ask how they might be able to escape the madness that's going on in the community. Or how can I elevate myself above the pain of rejection. Now, their parents can't help them grow up with the mindset that they need to get out and still maintain their restraint to run. Being wild growing up in this days and time is to run a race of uncommitted sorrows.

We live in a time when people guess on the goodness along with the character. His goodness can be defined as the collective perfection of His nature. I shoot dope for twenty something years and the only thing I found that helped me was love of God. Now, I knew that you don't want to hear this but its true. I think that the reason it won't work is that you won't let it work. You got to think clean, there's no way around this truth.

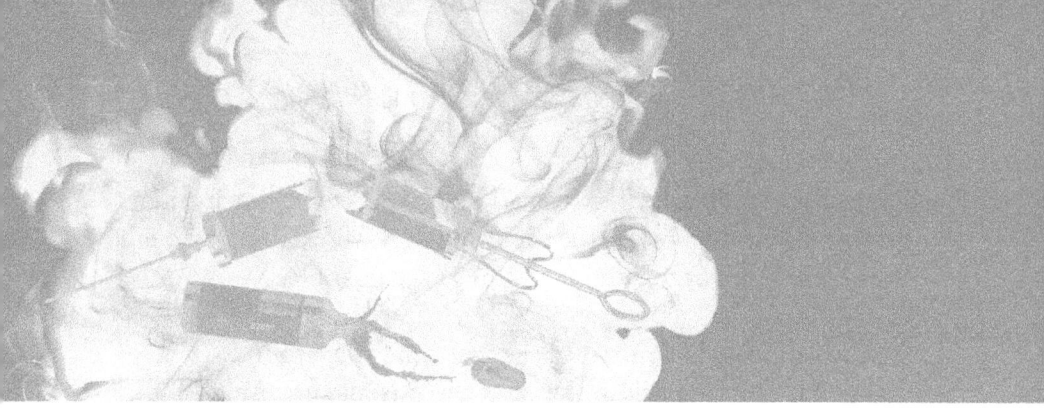

PRAYER FOR STRENGTH

Father, I thank you. I believe this young man has been through years of drug abuse and I believe him. But Lord, I am trusting in you to help me and others to give us strength to overcome this madness. Lord, I know in my heart that you didn't make me to do these things to my body and mind.

Father, these drugs destroys one's will. Give me strength to say no because I just can't. Lord, help those that want to be helped. Like me, I know they are tired too. They may not want to admit this but they are tired of waking up not being able to do anything until pills are taken or dope is shot. Lord, help me to overcome this weakness. Help us with this mental disorder, I know that you made us to be dependent on one but you. So thank you Father, in the name of Jesus.

I know that it maybe said what's the use. But they are only gone. Do the same thing after the thirty days.

Now, I think that a lot of people know about the power of God. But in order for them to stay current with the boys or girls. They deny any association, it's like one time I was standing on the block after being out all day stealing. And I looked up and seen my mom on the back of a Harley Davidson. I didn't want to believe it but my brother-in-law had his on the back, and they were balling through the block. You got to believe all things are possible.

The word lives. My mom was at that time was around seventy-years-old. On the back of that hog she was just grinning. But in getting back, you must trust Jesus and tell him about every time you feel like doing drugs or whatever.

Since I've been on this earth, I've gathered that this America is the greatest whatever you want. If there is enough that want the same thing is to put it to a vote.
But in my opinion, there are some things that don't need to be voted on. Like the laws that were established at the beginning. Now, everything has been challenged. Even God himself, the Holy Spirit, and even Jesus Christ as well as the ceremonials, attributes of his character. But then if you step back and bear witness, you will know that since the beginning, Satan has done almost anything to belittle Jehovah Tsidkenu's father.

Help us to know and believe that you are the only Eleazar in our Life. Thank you.

Allow God to talk to you like he talked to Job, read Job:38 and start at the first verse.

Let me tell you, we need a savior in our life. We are under constant pressure from parents, from peers, from friends, the police. Nowadays we need the Church in unmasking the Demonic Protocols through the Church to help us realize and recognize the oppressions of Satan's resources for victory. We live in a beautiful world yet to survive we must know our real enemies. Our strong enemies are not people but invisible forces of darkness which manipulate good into doing bad things. Especially those

THE BEGINNING... THE END... ANEW!

in charge of the snares and chains. Keeping us captive to wrong living, wrong thinking, wrong decisions, and wrong relationships. All to hold people down and keep us from discovering our way home. Freedom will be clearly seen in the life of individuals or in the life of liberated people.

Some people who are free from the enemy's strongholds experience an amazing awakening to spiritual life. But never have I seen a more joyless person than the average religious gathering of people restrained and bound by tradition demonition, as well as pride.

All those who follow Christ or profess to be Christians to train themselves for war, they will not see a moral revolution. Now can we stop the erosion of our own western culture without a spiritual fight. An increasingly militant Islam will not stop it's advances unless the Church takes the truth empowered by the Holy Spirit into battle.

The victory is ours but we must enforce it. God promises revival and a harvest to those who come home from bondage. The life of an addict is defeat. As I set my pen again to this subject I do so with the battle scars of a seasoned veteran. I have learned much on the battle front that must be shared for those that want to take the battle to the next level. Are you ready? It is time to allow the Lord to train us to reign.

There is something wrong in our world that cannot be explained by human reasoning. Unfortunately, most of the world, especially our western society, has rejected the idea that a supernatural evil has control of people that don't believe in nothing or nobody. But Christians have no choice but to face the fact that scriptural historical and even contemporary fact. That we are fighting a supernatural enemy, we must have a healthy recognition and knowledge of our enemy and I am not talking about the one with a pitch folk and red tail either.

Father in the name of Jesus, help us with this mellow madness of mind and body. Lord help us to understand that you are our security in this life and the life to come. Give wisdom to those that are charged with finding a cure for whatever, Father help us. With itchy ears send someone like minded so to help me understand your word, Lord. Bless everyone that call on the name of Jesus. Give them understanding when it comes to their love one's, Father. These things I ask in the name of Jesus.

Maybe this book will help those that want to help themselves and give them insight as to how to go about this process. I've been there.

God Bless.

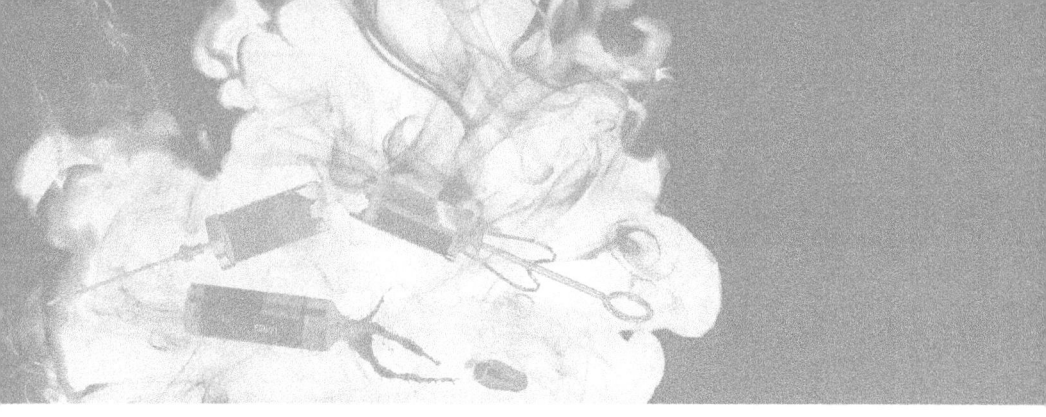

A FEW WORDS OF WISDOM FROM THE AUTHOR

God said you shall be holy for I, the Lord your God, am holy. Sin becomes sin when measured against God's standard. One reason sin is sin is because we have a low view of God and his standard. Look, I beg you to present your bodies a living sacrifice holy and pleasing to God. This is your spiritual act of worship. Do this, try to stop sinning and study the Bible, that's all I am asking you. I'll handle the rest.

Let God be God

Shanon Beach
919-6825-6174

PART 5

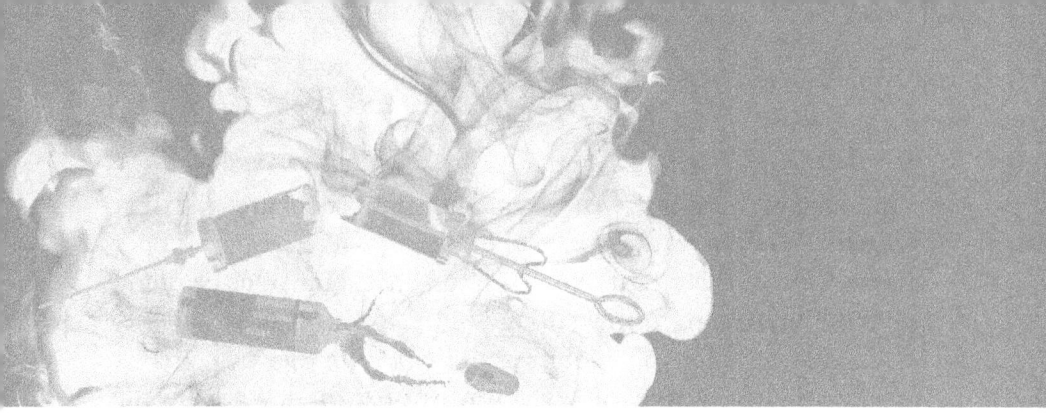

You know an unforeseen ability most of us process is the knowledge of purpose. Good or bad. When it comes to helping ourselves, we tend to be rate ourselves with reasons why we should or should not perform a certain task. If it will help us instead, we run from the very help we need no matter how important it is to us. As a group or as an individual.

There's good in each of us. But there's also evil in all of us. Rejection often times gives us new directions and refusing to accept the fact that we are little fishes trying to stay afloat in the sea of forgiveness. Swim little fish swim. Only give heed to yourself, and keep your soul diligently so that you do not forget the things which your eyes have seen. They do not depart from your heart all the days of your life.

But make them known to your son and your grandsons. Now, I think that the teachings about our savior stopped with our father's. They stopped seeking truth about God so they couldn't really teach us about the trusting in God's presence and love. One need to navigate these waters for that favor the wickedness of the old man and the accolades of this world.

Speaking of this world, we read and hear from our church folk that Satan or Lucifer or the prince of darkness, whichever you prefer is the God of this world. Now, it seems that some of us be doing everything we can to stick around in this world that we can see. But I got news for you people, we were born to die. Of course it really depends on what or which way we go up or down. Now my Bible tells me that you got to know where you are at.

No matter which way you go, I hate pain. Especially if it's going last any length of time. The Bible says that it's a forever situation with hell. Faith is the confident assurance of things hoped for. Can you imagine if we don't change our ways.

I was really dumb founded about God one time as all of us be one time refusing to except the fact that God is God and that we are just little fishes trying to stay afloat in this sea of forgiveness trying to stay afloat is somewhat hard to do when there are fishes all around you wanting to gobble you up and the ones that don't want to be gobble you up will try anything to get you to run with them but they know that you can't swim as well so you fall behind get lose and even promise crazy things that you can't deliver on and then you start falling into the abyss a depth in which no one can reach you

But now if you happen to fine someone or a group that care you should allow them to cast the net on the right side now one may ask why on the right side

Remember in the beginning when God gave man the right to rule and govern. That power when the Lord told the disciples to cast their net on the right side, at that moment he gave them authority. Our creation, or to fish, and after the ascension. He gave us that same power. That's what a lot of us refuse to do but it is mandatory meanwhile, we must study the word of God. First, we must believe

THE BEGINNING... THE END... ANEW!

every word in the Bible no matter if we think it makes sense or not. We must believe there may be a lot of reason. People will say and are saying that why not to conform to Christianity and one of the most replied answer is, I don't need God.

How can one say that they don't need the God of the universe. Man has an idea of an infinite or perfect being, only a fool will fall in a state of denial. With a heart hardened by likeminded and bizarre thinking of a wicked person.

Now, when something happens to people they say where was God? He's there, he's always been on the throne or more important on his throne. Remember, there's no one beside him but bad things happen to people to see if they are going to call on the Lord in time of need.

Obey me fully, this is what I want from my creation. Contentment and obedience bridging the holiness gap. And when you think you have fallen short that's when you call on the name of the Lord Jesus, my son. But first except him as Savior.

Everything that is happening in the world today is manmade. I believe because of what has happen in the past, we are supposed to be good stewards of the land, air, forest, everything. That we have been in trusted with on this earth. Unfortunately, a lot of us think that we run something, even God like most of us do. I am just trying to keep it real. Some of us at one time or another played God, in something you do act or say. You know you that but the Bible that I read says I am God. Isn't nobody up here with me? I am a bad man, I had to paraphrase a little. You understand, some arguments may not prove conclusively that God is in your mind. But they do show that in order to talk about the existence of knowledge, thought reason or conscience in man. We must assume that God is even. The Scripture announces the fact of

God's existence. I know that God is because for over twenty-something years I shoot drugs, speeding drop in all kinds of pills, shooting dope with dirty needles, getting water out of toilets to find my dope and most of the time there was still blood inside the syringe. So you can't tell me about the figment of your imagination that keeps you from forming a mental image of something or someone greater than myself.

It may sound crazy but it's out of love that I share this information with you. People like you that wants to escape the little waves of life's misguided illusions. You may say why do the bible say that God has hands and feet. Well, I was taught that this is the only way that a lot of people could relate and you will learn more about this as you study his word. As you study the bible, you will learn that he's bigger than anything that you can imagine. I think that a lot of folks just don't realize his bigness. God loves this world of sinners and ungodly men and women because we are the objects of his love. Now the human race and the world at large is the reason why Jesus died on the cross. If you don't believe that, then I am sorry. And as a friend of mine use to say, sorry is a sorry word.

We seem to forget that the Lord said that we are not fighting against flesh and blood. This is a spiritual battle and I don't care how bad you think you are. You can't do nothing with something you can't or don't want to see. The doctrine of and unity of God does not exclude the idea of the plurality of a person. I believe that there are however three persons in God. Nevertheless, there's only one God.

With the doctrine of the trinity, the analysis is it's a deep mystery which cannot be fathomed by our finite mind, but only taught in scripture as it does not warrant reasonable doubt. This is a doctrine which must be believed without doubt.

THE BEGINNING... THE END... ANEW!

The bible says that above all we must believe. But most of all, or some time, we trust in a pill, or a needle, or a joint, or anything we feel that will numb us to the reality of life, which will change us to a desirable condition obtained from a waste product. A byproduct obtained solely for to alter one's mind.

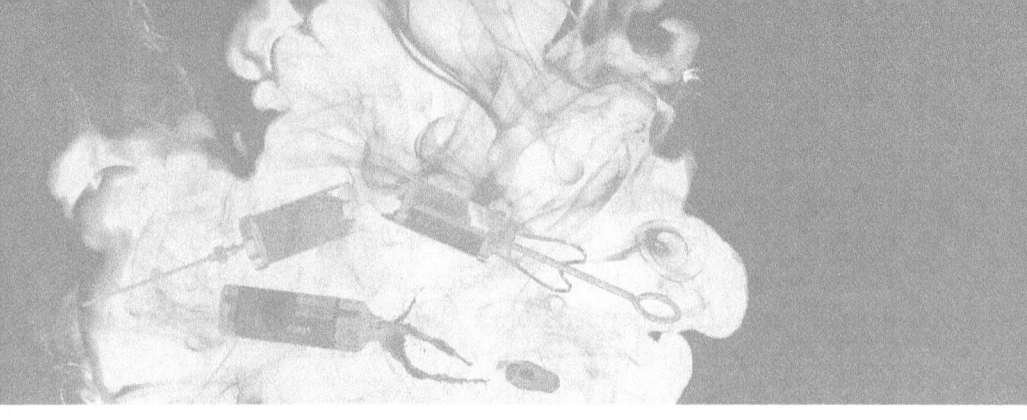

LET'S PRAY

Lord I'm asking a prayer of intercession for my brothers and sisters that have lost hope and think that all has been lost to intervals of unbelief in self. Father, help them see that all is not lost to humanism. That mankind supersedes all creation. That mankind is more than conquerors. In Christ, help them see that the only answer to their problems is with you Lord. Help them make a conscience and the dedicated decision to allow you free reign in their life. Lord, rejuvenate their mind toward righteousness so that they can relate and have a meaningful relationship with you. See the attributes of your holiness, let them see that when their name is coupled with that of God the father that it implies equality which in most cases is far removed when it comes to mankind. Lord give them holiness but most of all give them the will to accept and do your will in the name of Jesus.

I am blessed to know when someone asks questions pertaining to the mind of Christ. The Lord, if you want to know what he says about anything, read his word through the Bible. This should surely surmount any notion you have about how you think he should run his creation. Don't you think he can save you from anything that would hinder you from accepting him as Lord. His word will purge your mind, rehabilitate your soul, and reinstate

THE BEGINNING... THE END... ANEW!

your spirit. God can do anything. The highest ruler in the kingdom of man, he giveth it to whom so over he will. Know that satanic forces are most dominant in the disobedience of man. Trust me.

The support group of mine is my family. It's been some years since I was delivered from drugs, but from time to time the evil one will try to trip you up with dreams. That's when you need to talk to someone in your group that understands you, and what you have been through or is going through. The longer that you've been free the more realistic the dream. But when it happens you need to talk to somebody preferably the Lord.

I want you to keep in this mind the blessing of adaption. We were not meant to change God's message. God's message is meant to change us.

We need to realize that God is creator and with Jesus name is coupled with that of the father. I believe that a lot of things which are happening now is because your parents. Forget who brought them from the fields, I made someone listen and put compassion in place. I am asking you to come to me cast and your troubles on me. I can handle them I am your Father. I want and will give you the best of everything. All I ask is that you be obedient to my word and trust in my son and believe.

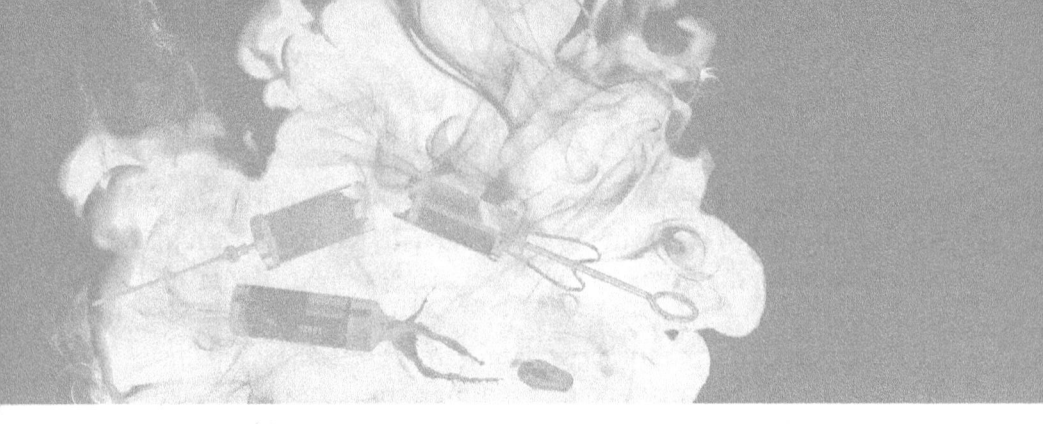

THE GOD OF THIS WORLD

The God of this world has blinded the minds of them which believe that Satan is not only the object of this world's worship, but he is also the moving spirit of its goddess activities. He's bad that he got people thinking that God is not God, that your better-half should be another man. I believe that people that go against God's order are looking for standards of truth that are lose. In the body of lies formulated in their mind isn't hurting nobody, or I am grown I can do what I want to and be looking for morsels of truth. For a spiritual meal, moreover they think that they can raise kids. The same way as their minds are lacking and being muzzled by its unbelief. It's bewitch by the God of this world, the standard by with we must live is the standard put forth by the Creator.

Unsure we live in a time when God's very existence is in question by some. Now there are some that thinks it was the big bang. For some, we came from apes and others the sea. Then there are those that say that God isn't God, that all this just happens. I am here to help you understand.

One of God's infinite attributes is his character in which I believe that his wrath is coupled with compassion. If not so, then I think

THE BEGINNING... THE END... ANEW!

that he would just take you out. But let's not forget that salvation is his ultimate goal for mankind.

When you proclaim Jesus as Lord you must deny the world view of disillusioned righteousness. In which this or some people seem to think is right.

This country is in trouble. We were founded on the pillars and the fundamental laws of conduct. but there has been the igniting of an explosive device call pride and the very breath you need to deny God comes from God.

The church is dying on its feet instead of praying on its knees. If you are exposed to an idea long enough it becomes normal. What will we gain when we lose, it's time to stand for our reform. The environment conforms to us like a school. In form, prison is supposedly to reform us. But only Christ can transform us. The greatest trusting you can do for your soul is to accept God.

A dangerous position for a heartrending society, some of the problem is that the destruction of people is engulfed in the minds of those that have forgotten the savior. They thought they had the upper hand by keeping people oppressed, tricked, and thinking that if they half-heartedly give people some of what they want. A little at a time, some of the time now. The bible says that this is an untoward generation, but not a senseless one. Somebody woke up and still waking up to mistrust and misuse of the powers entitled to them by the standard supposedly entrusted to them.

Jehovah - Jira: The Lord will provide
Jehovah- Rapha: The Lord of health
Jehovah- Nissi: The Lord over banner
Jehovah- Shalom: The Lord our peace
Jehovah- Ra-ah: The Lord my Shepherd

Jehovah- Tsidkena: The Lord our righteousness
Jehovah- Shammeh: The Lord is present

Moreover, the personal pronouns ascribed to God prove personality, is a sharp distinction that's drawn in the scriptures. Between the Gods of the heathen and the Lord God of Israel, idols are things not persons. They cannot walk, speak, do good or evil. God is wiser than the men who made these idols.

Lord, help me to read this from a spiritual standpoint as intended by the author. God, when I accept your son as my Lord and savior, I want you to be with me every time I think that I want to get high. I need for you to help me with the fear of living straight a life. Strengthened by the knowledge of your life and word.

Now friend, when this happens you will never be the same. God is your supplier, Jesus is his lieutenant and the Holy Spirit is his enforcer, in that order.

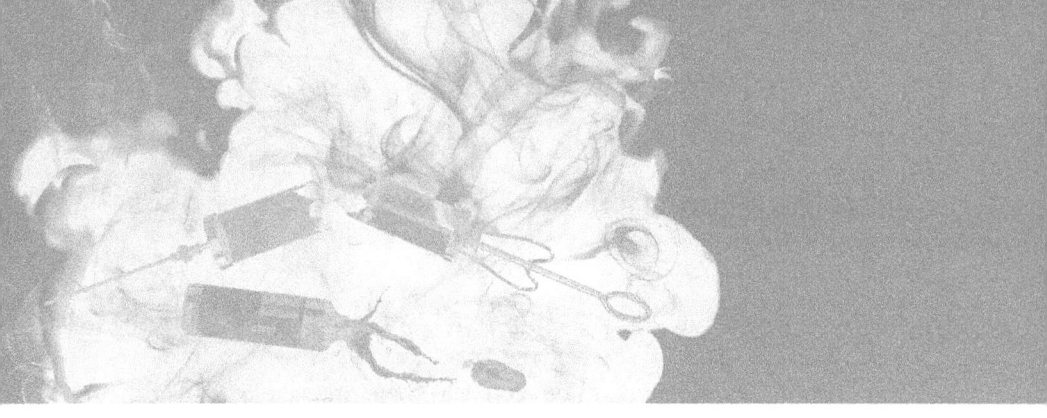

DANGEROUS POSITION

There can be no half-hearted position of trust. God must be your priority, the first fruit of everything that he blesses you with, you need to give it to God. And if you don't you enter, man will suffer. Lost and for a while you will need to take a seat at the table of brokenness.

There is nothing that will save you for God but God. How Jesus is and when you except him as Lord, at that very moment, you are fit for the kingdom.

Now everybody can't say that they be waiting on false Gods, manmade gods with no power except to tear down the body and mind and tricking you into laying your soul bare to the wicked one. Entrusting your mind to the God of this world stretched or extended beyond its normal limits. But God will not allow you to sit at the table of brokenness.

We are talking about why this happen or that happened. But those of us that are over forty- years must know and teach our younger folk that Jim Crow isn't dead. It's just flying a little higher. How many of you know that we as a people, and especially a child of God, must mount up on wings of eagles. Where we fly even higher that my friend, can only be achieved through the person of Jesus Christ.

There's nobody so good that they don't need Jesus. Also, nobody is so bad that God can't save them. Because it's your nature that takes you places, that won't help you. Only the message of Jesus can change us. A lot of people would say my mother or my father has enough church for both of us but know this, every knee shall bow and every tongue shall confess. It's on you, not father or mother.

The first thing we need to do is admit to our condition go to the Lord. In prayer, confess your sins and believe in your heart that God raised him from the dead. You will be saved.

Now this is not something that can be garnered by self. This is a free gift no matter what you've done or anything like that. Now, from the beginning, he gives all of us a little bit of faith. Everybody know about this God I serve, but then he tells us that faith comes by hearing. I would say that this faith in the beginning is to help you in your disbelief. As you go about your way, while you make up your mind to do the right thing. Because only in the Bible can any satisfying light is found on the mystery and baffling subjects of life, and death. However, differences between the two makes it clear that the terms are not identical. The kingdom of God can only be entered by the new birth of self, and only Christ has the keys.

I spoke earlier about God's grace. Now, this Grace is only possible to us. You and me because of the love the son has for the father. Remember, God dislike for sin. It is like trying to get oil and water to mix but we know that the oil has one function and water has another, and together they only make a mess. But Christ's death on the cross freed God up to shower us with His grace. Back in the day when God was with the people and they did something wrong, he withheld hid forgiveness and his wrath was inescapable. Because

THE BEGINNING... THE END... ANEW!

the bible says he looked away and at that time his wrath, I believe, had free course in your life. Speaking of his wrath, is characteristic called wrath would render the study of him incomplete. God's wrath must be taken as his righteous retribution against sin.

God must judge sin although he takes no pleasure in punishing the unrighteousness. We find no way around it, nowhere can one hide from the coming event. When you wish to be a child of the king, if you want to enter into the family of the most high, you must submit. Because there is no escaping, but it won't be that bad. My yoke is easy and my burden is light. It isn't that bad. Don't be afraid of your past so there will be no fear when God tells you about your future. Right now, I believe that God has most of us in a holding pattern. Until the winds of your former life subside, prayer is you asking God to intervene in your situation.

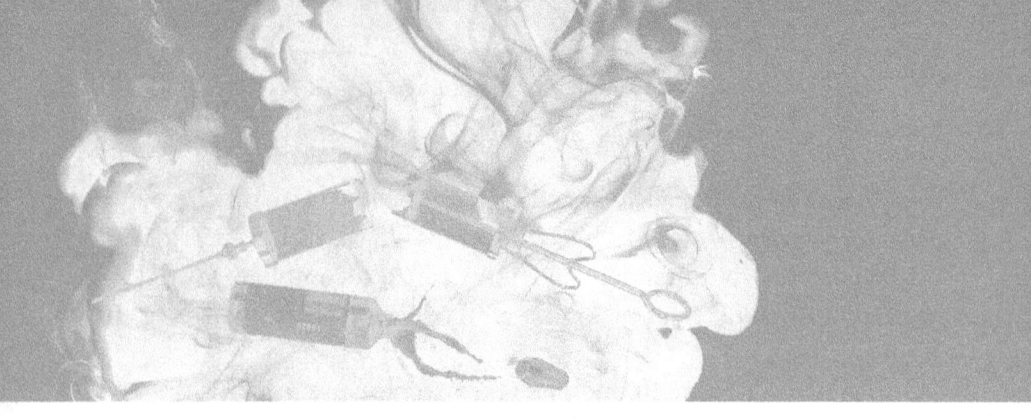

IT STARTS AT HOME

In the past, and I am certain that in the future. If God don't intervene, our youth will continue to be lost. Why? Because they refuse to learn of the only hope for them, their parents. The world as we know it, a lot of them don't know God and are not interested in his teaching. They are too ashamed to ask their parents. Not that they would know who this God or the Bible is.

Their minds held captive by anything that oppose the teaching and lifestyle of Jesus Christ. I've noticed when a lot of young folks are discouraged with life, as they know it. When it seems that nothing is working. They more often than not, turn to the bottle and think that if they can drink enough, that their problems will go away. It seemed they do until you stop drinking or get drunk. But this drinking only enslaves your mind and entrap you to a life of dependence and delusions. Then your fall into the eternal curse of denial and then you say to self, at least I am not on drugs.

But dead is dead. There is no half measure when you are dead. You being done isn't not coming back. God isn't no recycling God. I don't think so.

THE BEGINNING... THE END... ANEW!

The bible doesn't say anything about drinking, it says don't get drunk. But now I drink in some cases. You drunk now, I think that anything that alters you mind, your body functions you don't need, you may as well you did drugs. For a long time, you don't know well. I also sold liquor most of my life. Also it's bad for you or for your health. Everything about it is just bad.

Especially for young people because their little brains are mostly affected. Even thought about life. You're not even at the age where you think you know what you want for yourself. And you are already on lowdown with low key psychiatric disorders. What a shame, you had such a bright future and now you only got brain development problems. Everything that go with it, you tend to have less interest in activities. Your appearance takes a shot. You begin to not care about how you look, and everything and people will only see you as a dirty underage drinker with oversized problems. Look, all these treatment centers and stuff won't get you where you need to be. You can't send a Ferrari to a Buick dealer and expect it to run normal. Think about this for a minute, cut out the drugs and alcohol.

Alcoholism, the chemistry of drinking allows alcohol to affect nearly every type of cell in the body. Including those in the central nervous system. Not being able to meet work, school, or family responsibilities. That is if you so stop it, if you need help, pray.

When you attend these programs and the likes, the first thing you or whoever you do is grab a cup of coffee and pile it with full of sugar. It doesn't get where you want to go. But there's caffeine effects like jitters, restlessness, nervousness, anxiety, and you put four or five packs of sugar and you off to the races. But you only taste it good but after a long time you will feel the effects. So you only switch one high for another. The other just take a longer time to affect your body and after a time you can't do without it. Got to have it no matter what. First thing we can't go our whole life depending on the way that substance, any substance can make you feel. That's not normal.

Normal is waking up in the morning and giving thanks to God. For him, and nobody else. Taking you out and recognizing him as the creator and Lord. that's normal.

Now, in the eventful time you find time to come around. Think for yourself without the benefit of drugs, you need to help yourself and those that love you and pray for you from afar. Start giving thanks for them and realize whose world this is.

Everything that's happening happened because people are forgetting God and not thanking Jesus. This may seem a little harsh but it's a true bill none the less. Whoever owns the father of the family more than often owns the family. Because the father knows that he's the head. No matter which road he decides to travel, more often than not, the son will follow as well. As the daughter because she loves dad and mom, don't want to see the family break up. So she will often follow for little while.

Now to be infused with the treats of a father is a good thing. But if he forfeits that right, this superficial world will forever remind the son of the state of a continuous change. And he must keep up or be gobbled up by false motives that's intended to destroy him, his belief, and the beat goes on. So we must get with the program.

The problem is especially with us people of color is that we don't really have a legacy to pass down. To pass down to our sons and daughters. Especially spiral and black people are spiritual if nothing else. Material things only last a little while but if we pass along spiral knowledge, this will last a lifetime. I think that this is why we don't have foundation in a lot of our communities

THE BEGINNING... THE END... ANEW!

because nobody wants to learn about Jesus and leave a legacy for spiritual growth. To be passed down from father to son or daughter. Remember, nothing from nothing leaves nothing.

I was raised in a liquor house. But I will never forget God and also knew Jesus as Lord and still had to act as man of the house. Because there was not legacy passed down telling me that I need to take some time and recognize where my strength comes from. But you know, God draw's you in his own time.

The ability of man to overcome is that he knows the process is. The fact and knowledge of a gradual change to physically overcome any obstacle set before him. But that bit of power is dwarfed by a little power. That pill, that smoke, and anything that alters one's mindset can only be conquered through the knowledge of one's spiritual venture with Christ. In which a new birth is the only thing that will enable you to claim victory over the unseen spirits call drugs.

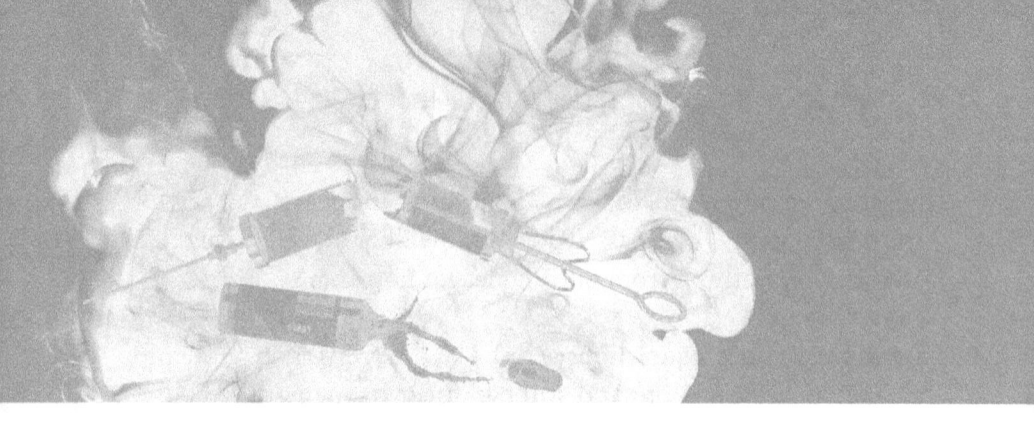

LET'S PRAY.

Father, I thank you for helping with this affliction of my mind and body. Lord, in the name of Jesus, I thank you. Thank you for keeping me in my right mind, thank you for keeping me in my right mind, thank you for helping me to see that there is no other God beside you father. I give you praise, honor, and glory. For you are a healer and keeper and I thank you in the name of Jesus.

You know I shot dope for a long time. Opium, crack, anything that I could shot in my arm. But after a while if you don't OD, first you get tired of everything. You begin to think about this isn't what we were created for. Look, only God can help you overcome this madness. First and foremost you must want to stop waking up in the morning asking yourself where will I get some dope from today. Or worry about getting a water shot from your so called partner. There is no honor with addicts. The Lord helps us to get rid of this life stealing want. Help us in the name of Jesus. I am tired. Thank you in Jesus name.

God made you whole from the beginning but somehow along the way you created an open wound in your soul. And the only doctor that can help you close this wound is God through Jesus with the help of the Holy Spirit.

THE BEGINNING... THE END... ANEW!

Now that's a true bill. You never expected to become an addict but anything in this world that will help the tempter captures your soul. He will use mostly physical dependence. A lot of times, he will speak into your mind and have you go to a school or your work place and shoot it up and kill people. And if you don't get killed by the police, you get put in his factory of misfits until the action of destroying can begin again. Help us Lord not to go to any factory of misfits. You said in your word that you are a keeper

If we don't lend our kids to faith in God, you lead them to have faith in the culture which is trying to destroy them. Most of us don't know anything about faith because our parent didn't know about faith.

One of the greatest gifts God gave us is the freedom to make choices. But those options always bring about consequences good or bad. But God is waiting for us to make a choice of faith in God.

I'm trusting that the Lord will use the messages in this book to take your faith to the next level. In him, insecurities, faults, and frailties, are occasion's to fulfill the destiny of God for your life.

Lord, help me with the defect of character, these are character traits that will help you along the way.

Compassion – investing in whatever is necessary to heal the hurts of others.

Discernment - understanding the deeper reasons why things happen.

Dependability - fulfilling what I consented to do even if it means unexpected sacrifice.

Diligence - investing my time and energy to complete a task assigned to me.

Endurance - the inward strength to withstand stress and do my best.

Generosity - carefully managing my resources so I can freely give to those in need.

Gratefulness - letting others know by my words and actions how they have benefitted my life.

Humility - acknowledging that achievement and results from the investment of others on my life.
Obedience - quickly and cheerfully carrying out the direction of these who are responsible for me.

Meekness - yielding my personal rights and expectations with a desire to serve.

These are a couple of character traits that will help you no matter what

These are defects that everyone need to work on

Anger	Pride
Honesty	Laziness
Greed	Impatience
Grandiosity	Punctuality
Forgiveness	Gratefulness
Faith	Profanity
Procrastination	Irresponsibility
Dependency	Lust
Envy	Close-mindedness

THE BEGINNING... THE END... ANEW!

We need to become entirely ready to have God. Remove all of these defects of character and it will happen little by little. Because God is spirit working on your spirit. You won't even notice. Also these cast of character defects will hinder the best laid plans for recovery from addiction of any kind. We to must also make an effort to intentionally minimize the defect that we are so fond of.

He is the prince of this world who hath blinded the minds of them that believe. Not there is doubtless an allusion. Here in this world of evil spirits and is organized and that Satan is at the head of the children of disobedience. Our temptation is said to come from three sources, the world, the flesh, and the devil. As some naturalist would say there is always this damming fact that remains when were born in sin.

What's so good about this is we don't have to stay in sin. There's a lot of ways to avoid this madness. Even though we were born in it, a lot of folks just don't do a lot of foolish stuff. But now, that's just for their body but not their mind.

Even though your body may seem clear and clean, your mind will not allow this process to go forward on its own. For this to happen, we must admit and accept the fact that this process can only be done by someone bigger that you can imagine. You know.

Even though we accept Christ, he will ask you to renew your mind through his word. But even then it will take a little while on your part it's already done. As far as Christ is concerned.

I was listening to the word of God days ago and afterward I stopped and thought about some of the thing's going on in society. People being killed because of this or that. But then it makes you think about everything going on outside our borders. When we should be worried about the things going on inside in your community.

My community, it seems like there's to it only. Sometimes even in the Church, and it seem like God isn't everywhere. He is supposed to be named in the hearts. They believed and it let them without wonder that's within as it lets you know that some people love God, but they deny the power of they don't wait to get it. Faith is determined by movement. If there is no movement, there is no faith. But it comes by hearing the word of God.

Evil things are everywhere but it seems that this one group are so evil that people from all over the world want to be part of their demise. Amazing, there's drug hitting us on one side with our babies. And then there are those that want to tell God how he should run his world. There are people that think they can take other people stuff with no consequence and then there's the police killing people just because. People getting shot because they don't look like people think. They should be handcuffed in back of police car, shot himself in the head for not paying toll to ride train. Shot to death. Hands up don't shoot!

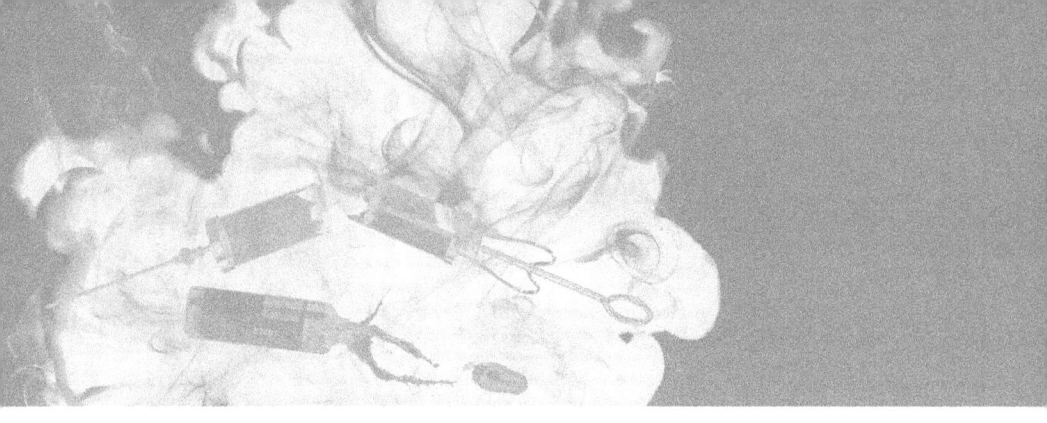

WHAT MUST THE CHURCH SAY?

THE IDEAS AND NOTIONS OF mankind has dwarfed the laws of man, and the commands of God which was completed in the beginning.

But along the way, complications arose and arguments ensued and everybody wanted to be the head. That's not the way it was intended. If you don't believe me, ask God.

I made man and then woman. I made the man to be in control and for you to not obey me, you are telling me to my face that I am a lie. I didn't make a man and woman, the female is the only being that I made to have offspring. Everything that comes against God was composed by a people that disavow the laws of man and the commandments of God.

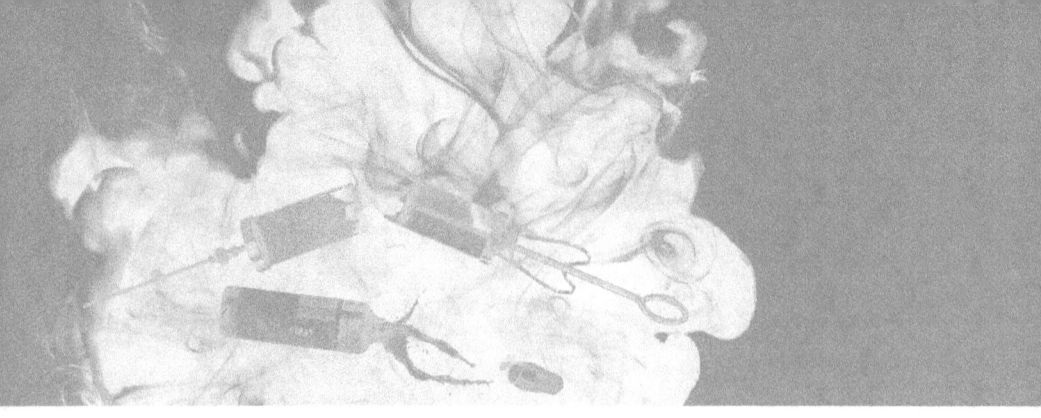

GET FREE

Wow I am pretty sure that there were no any extraordinary births other than the man and that woman was made from man's side.

Now, I believe that the Bible would have said so. I am a Christian and as such I am compelled to speak against sin anywhere, anytime, anyplace. That's the gospel.

I believe that to be factious about anything other than God's creation. I think would be doing a disservice to the faith and that's not normal.

Now, if you want to turn yourself around and do the hokie-pokie, that's on you. But as for me, and my house, I don't think that it is very healthy to be hostile to the God of the Bible.

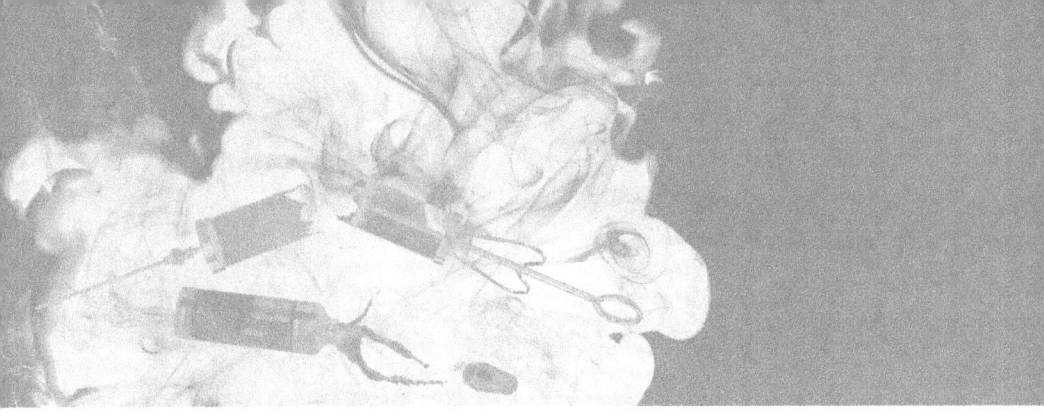

TOP OF THE PILE

W E AS A PEOPLE ARE accustomed to being at it or near the top of the heap no matter the situation.

Location or condition are not lucid to the fact the we need Jehovah-Jireh to help us through this world of indifference. This world of carnality where people think that they can tell the Creator how to right this world, that they could run better. We as a people have been and still are being persecuted. For so little that when we see the light at the end of the turnpike, we think that it's because of something we said or done. Don't trip.

Truth. The bible present Jesus as the Godman in a human body. The bible is like no other book in the world. It impacts individuals, cultures, whoever engages in its message. Teaches truth about man, creation, sin, salvation, any subject it touches. Only the Bible teaches history in advance. Also talks about the issue, truth that is inescapable and how it can be applied to our everyday life without bias.

Everyone who is of the truth hears my voice. Now, if you are not interested in truth you are interested in God. When Jesus came on the scene he prayed and ask God to sanctify them in the truth. I believe he prayed this so you will be able to tell the difference.

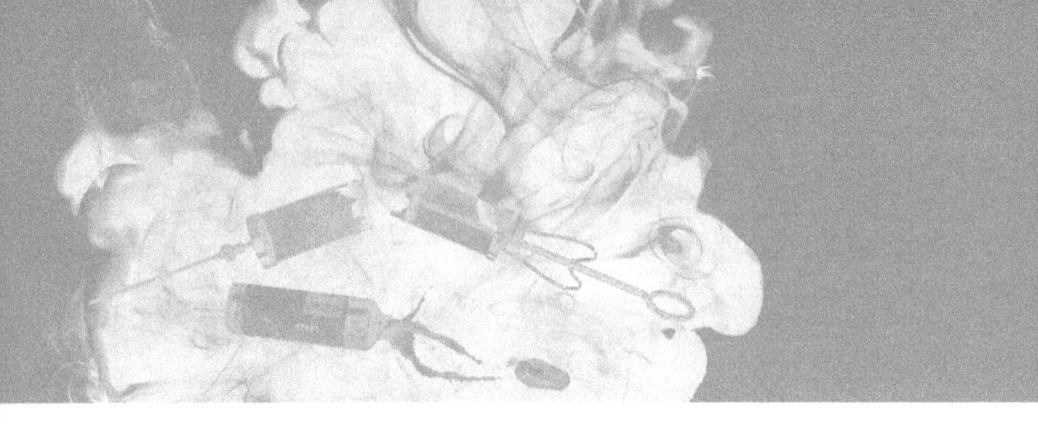

THANK YOU LORD SAVE OUR CHILDREN

W E NEED TO ADMIT THAT losing is a state of mind or condition to God. There's nobody that think that they are so good that they don't need Jesus. Also, there's nobody so bad that God can't save them.

Listen our nature will take us places that can't help us. And raising your child in this secular society will cause him or her to hide themselves from God. Also it will cause them to hunch their shoulders in doubt or uncertainty when confronted with the age old question; Is God real? Who helped you open your eyes this morning.

You think God is not real. Who helped you breathe the gift of life? When you are faced with overwhelming odds, who you going call? Don't think it will be the hulk. I think that for most, people when asked, would say they believe in God. But I don't think that they are talking about the God of the Bible.

This generation seem to be finished with this transcendent deity that can rearrange our priorities and help us deal with that horrid concept of sin in our lives.

THE BEGINNING... THE END... ANEW!

They choose instead to go shopping for a faith that has fragments of Christianity. Mixed with something else and at times their, concept of God becomes as diverse as the items at a shopping mall.

A sickness of our age is that we have or most of us have fit bodies, unstable minds, and vacant souls, and no intention of filling the void. We must derive or knowledge of God from the Bible alone. Not from personal preferences or experiences. God stands alone.

All other religions are flawed, and missed attempts of man to reach God through human effort results in the worshipped idols but are actually worshipping demons.

Satan uses temptation to lure people away from God and cause them to do evil with a spirit of perversion and immorality.

Ladies and gent's contemporary spirituality has been redefined. Can you imagine being committed to a religion that teaches that good and evil don't exist. That sickness is an illusion and forgiveness from God is unnecessary. People really think that this is a far-fetched situation.

In Singapore, seventeen ounces of marijuana or half an ounce of cocaine or heroin will be treated as traffickers and they they get hanged on the gallows.

In Iran, one of the most active executioners of drug offenders under the Islamic regime, up to five-hundred drug traffickers are executed. Every year, more than 10,000 narcotics traffickers and drug users have already been put to death in Iran in the past few decades.

In Saudi Arabia as with alcohol penalties for possession and consumption of illicit drugs are severe. From public flogging to harsh jail sentences, drug traffickers meanwhile get the same penalty as murderers and rapist such as public beheadings.

In the United Arab Emirates there's a scarier aspect of drug laws. People gets arrested for even an infinitesimal trace of any drug. Consider this, a Swiss national was sentenced to four four years in prison after a customs official at Dubai airport found three poppy seeds from a bread roll. This, after he ate a bun at a Bun in Heathrow Airport in London before his flight to Dubai.

So you see, the laws in this United States isn't nothing. just suppose we live in another country. But then, even if we don't get caught, most of the time there will be an overdose or someone will give you a hot shot. Drugs will make you greedier, there are times when I knew that I was getting a water shot. I just had to play it off and not put it in my arm or do something foolish before I put it in my arm.

I don't think that there is no place in this or any other town where drugs has not infested its society. Drugs are a luxury that's really in the past was only afforded people in gated communities. But in the past few years, the gates were open, the fence was crossed, and open warfare was declared on our young kids. There was a conclusion to a problem of long ago, and the way the sheets could be folded or thrown away.

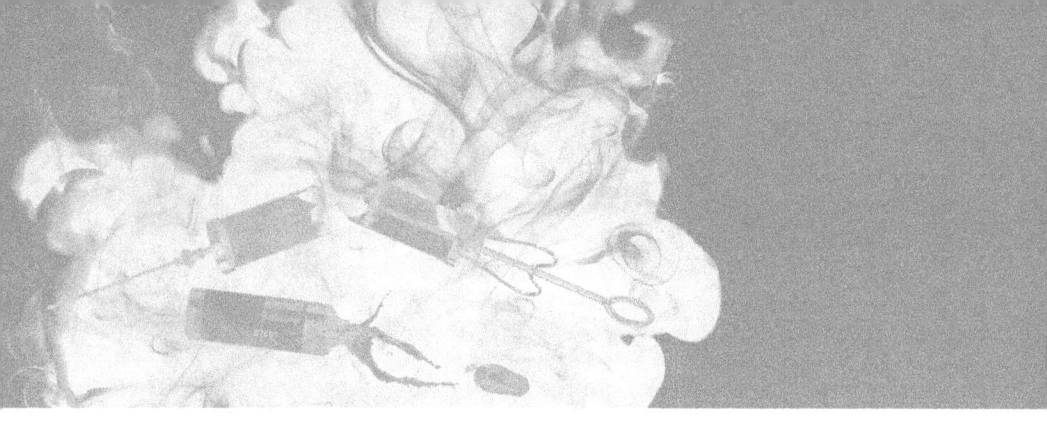

OUR DEFAULT POSITION AT CONCEPTION

Adam is the only one of God's creation that was born in a position of emptiness. After the fall, everybody was born with stuff already. With rebel in their memory, to be matured as we grow and rebel against God was on or at the top of the agenda.

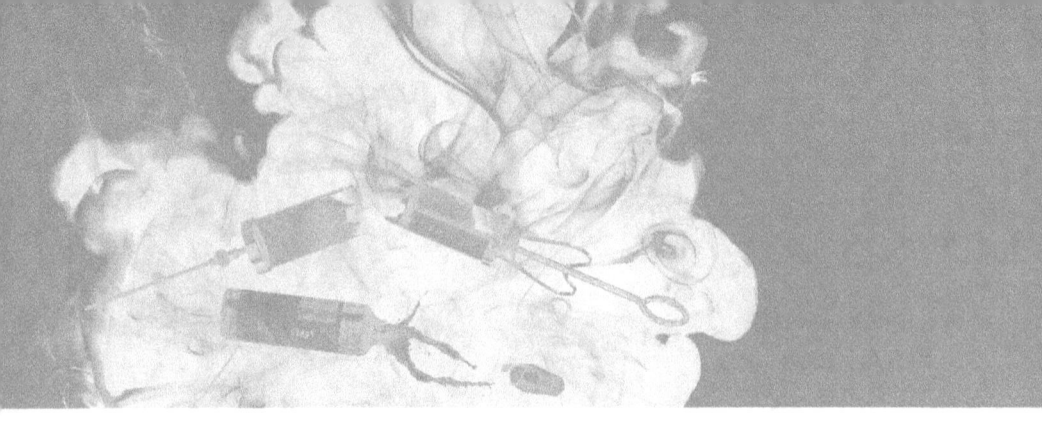

PASSING THE TORCH

It's amazing that people think that any personalities have the pre-conceived notion that life will happen regardless. But that's not an acceptable statement to make among persons. That study of life's road map for living and study the word of God.

Life's road map for living must be learned and be passed down. It's the right thing to do. Nevertheless, we don't need to worry about the wrong things. They come naturally because we were born in sin.

Now, when you've reached the intersection of expectation. After turning off the road of disappointment you will see that the right things that one learn from understanding. The right thing to do after being taught will help him or her. When encountering with the master, pass the torch but it must be lit with the fire of enthusiasm for God.

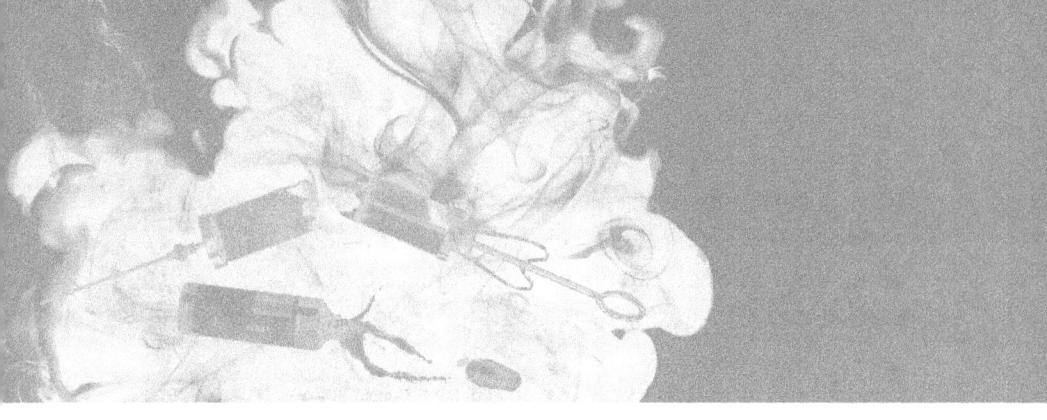

I WAS CRIPPLED

THE BIBLE SAYS THAT WE were born in sin, shaped in iniquities. This is what we had to look forward to from birth. Now your parents didn't know or else they would have taken you to church. Instead of sending you, they would have some of them helped you along. With the minister's help, you with living the Bible as well from the conception of one's birth. Until the real heartfelt separation from sin and iniquities.

Now from birth until separation you were a cripple even through you had two good leg's

We know that separation from sin can only come about if one has truly made up his or her mind. That they don't want to live like this anymore. Separation from sin is best done with a pure heart and made up mind. I thank God I am not a crippled anymore.

I was also crippled physically. I thought that the only way I could move normally is that I needed a shot of dope. I remember one time I was so sick that I just stuck the needle in my arm like I had some dope just to see the blood.

I thought that it made me feel better so you not only get high of the dope, you get high off seeing the blood and boot it like you are doing dope for real. I really was show. Just how sick dope or drugs take control of your mind and will make you believe anything.

Drugs have infected every aspect of our society. With no respect of person, color, or age. The younger the better, and we wonder why people are not taught who is in control. When we realize back in the day who was in control, those wasn't a lot of this madness going around.

Once upon a time, this young man I knew growing up was very envious and he wanted to be king of the hood. At the time, nobody would give this young man a chance. This young man was from and would do anything to get ahead. So he had all the people ahead of him set up for a life tour in the big house or they got dead.

Now, one of the most chilling things that could happen to someone is for him or her to be intimidated by someone they know is doing wrong. But they have big respect for them, and at some point or another, they have been hurt by society, or they fall into a bad financial situation and pride. But you know what they say, stuff happens.

That lifestyle will hurt any and everybody. You think you love starting with you?

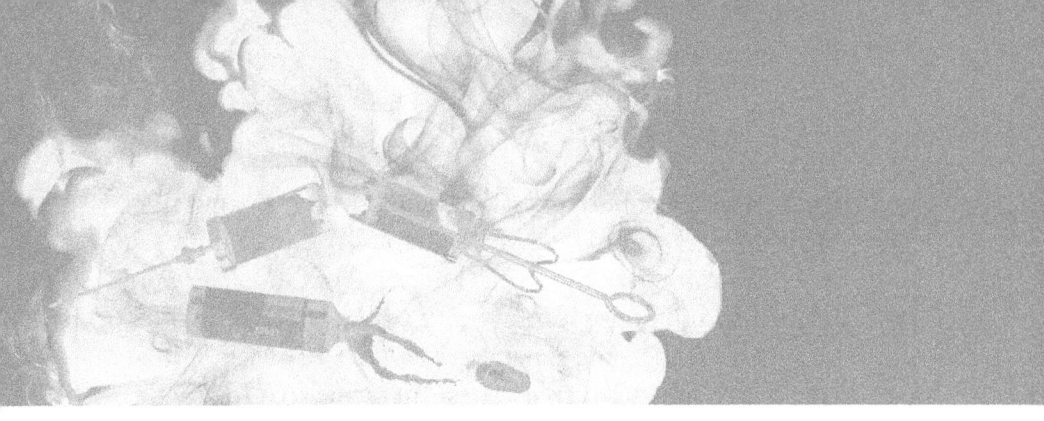

THE CYCLE MUST BE BROKEN

All too often fear helps us to be or do things were intended from the beginning. Fear helps us discover more of our cowardly self. If we happen to find something or someone to build our self-confidence, about anything we tend to cling to, that person or thing even through its effect contradicts our way or ways of living.

Say it isn't so. Well, I wish I could. But death comes slowly and that is something you can count on. Because we were born to die. How fast is up to you but it's going to happen and it can only be countermanded by God. So break the cycle of drugs in our lives and in our community.

One of the mysteries of life is not just to survive in this jungle of unfaithfulness to the God of the universe. Also, we as a people must adhere to the creator of time and space.

A God that's not a graven image of someone's imagination. The choice you make will determine if you will be a slave to somebody or something. The two most important days of your life is the day you were born and the day you find out why. Now there are a number of reasons why you were not born. You were not born to do drugs. You were not born to be a slave to anybody or anything. You were not born to Lord over your parents. You were not born to intentionally minimize the works and word of God. You were born to worship and praise him in every aspect of your life. He's not asking that you become super spiritual, but I am asking that you do try to live spiritually free as best that you can. God's word will teach you and his Holy Spirit will guide you.

I was an addict once. Then I learn to stop disrespecting myself and learned to respect Jesus as Lord. And he saved me from my powerful enemies, from those who hated me because they were too strong for me.

Thank you Lord in Jesus name.

We as a person can never be perfect. Outside of Christ perfection is something that has eluded us. As we envision perfection of self, along with thinking that you are a child of God.

Now there is a rude awakening awaiting in the wings to sock or bring you back to reality. Some of the most miserable people I know are active. Christians that love Jesus but deny the power of God.

The church must rediscover spiritual warfare. We must open our biblical and spiritual armory to force some people refuse to acknowledge.

Lord help my unbelief help me to see the problem at hand. And help us with life's most meaningful pursuit to destroy the misconceptions about spiritual warfare. In Jesus name.

You know you really should stop trying to drill a hole in water and realize that time is short. We need to stop cutting it short with

THE BEGINNING... THE END... ANEW!

drugs and whatever else that hinders the natural flow of life that was given to you by God.

One of the most underlying problems we face is greed. The next I believe is drugs, and the next I believe would be self-centerless. It's amazing.

We are all God's creation, we must act accordingly and channel that love where it belongs with the Lord Jesus Christ and not with allusions of the mind that alternate's self.

www.ingramcontent.com/pod-product-compliance
Lightning Source LLC
LaVergne TN
LVHW011947070526
838202LV00054B/4834